TABLE OF CONTENTS

ACRONYMS

ANA	Afghan National Army
ANP	Afghan National Police
ANSF	Afghan National Security Forces
AASLT	Air Assault
CSTC-A	Combined Stability and Training Command- Afghanistan
CSIS	Center for Strategic and International Studies
DRA	Democratic Republic of Afghanistan (1979-1992)
DoD	Department of defense
ETT	Embedded Training Team
FID	Foreign Internal Defense: Assistance to a foreign security force
GPF	General Purpose Forces
GIRoA	Government of the Islamic Republic of Afghanistan (2001-)
SGA	Small Group Advisor
IED	Improvised Explosive device
ISAF	International Security and Assistance Force
LLOC	Land Line of Communication
MMAS	Master of Military Arts and Science
NATO	North Atlantic Treaty Organization
ODA	Operational Detachment Alpha
SFA	Security Force Assistance
SF	Special Forces (Usually refers to US Army)
SOF	Special Operations Forces (Joint)
TRADOC	Training and Doctrine Command

CHAPTER 1

INTRODUCTION

Security Forces Assistance[1] is a linchpin of the military contribution to our

National Defense Strategy in the global counterinsurgency we are currently engaged in.

This invariably means that American soldiers are training foreign armies in Iraq,

Afghanistan, Pakistan, and Georgia, to name a few. Is it desirable or realistic to expect

that we can develop carbon copies around troubled spots that have different military

traditions and cultural ways of war? United States Field Manual 3-24, *Counterinsurgency*

advises us to "Avoid mirror imaging. That solution fits few cultures or situations"

(Department of the Army 2006a, Table 3-5). Doctrine in this case provides good advice

but as doctrine lacks detailed instruction of what mirror imaging could mean or where the

conflicts could arise. Doctrine is a general guideline that does not provide specific

guidance in all missions. This paper proposes to define the conflicts in mirror imaging

specifically in relation to the current attempt to stand up and strengthen the Afghanistan

National Army (ANA) by US military trainers and advisors, with a view to making

recommendations that will help overcome inherent cultural conflicts. The question is

what are the problem areas when merging two martial cultures when the US is training

the Afghan National Army?

This study focuses on the interaction between the United States Military and the

Afghan Security Forces. This is not to impugn the contributions from other ISAF forces,

---

[1]Security Forces Assistance: Unified action to generate, employ, and sustain local,
host nation or regional security forces in support of a legitimate authority (Joint Center
for International Security Force Assistance).

1

but to narrow the scope of research to a useable range. There are similarities between the US Military and other NATO forces, in particular British, German, or French units. However, this study considers each nationality to possess its own respective professional military subculture, even if it may share similarities with allies. Some extrapolation from this study can possibly be applied to the efforts of NATO Operational Mentor Liaison Teams (OMLT), but this study refrains from making any specific correlations.

The method of this study is to compare US and Afghan martial cultures. This comparison reveals contrasts in military practice and operation, revealing a variance in relative subculture values. This will suggest areas where an Afghan kandak or tribal lashkar may have difficulty absorbing a US professional model represented by their embedded trainers. These areas are predicted to cause US trainers to exert more effort in teaching their operating model. Alternately US trainers may help Afghans to modify their practice without violating core values.

It is commonly recognized that the development of strong host-nation security forces is one of the core requirements for a counterinsurgency strategy. US counterinsurgency doctrine lists host nation security forces as a recommended logical line of operation (LOO), and later stresses the importance of this goal because ultimately 'The host nation must secure its own people" (Department of the Army 2006a, 5-40). The ability to provide security to the populace is the first indicator of government legitimacy listed out of a possible six (Department of the Army 2006a, 1-116).

"While FID has been traditionally the primary responsibility of the Special Operations Forces, training foreign forces is now a core competency of regular and reserve units of all services" (Department of the Army 2006a, 6-12). Embedded Training

Teams (ETTs) of US General Purpose Forces (GPF) are the primary agent of training and supporting the ANA in Afghanistan. How effective are these teams at transferring US military prowess to soldiers who are much different in social organization, warrior ethos, and technical ability? On average, these teams have two months of language, cultural, and tactical training to prepare for a year-long embed with an Iraqi or Afghan battalion, in addition to any experience that each individual naturally brings to the team (US DoD Inspector General 2009, 45).

A primary assumption underlying this study is that training teams will primarily fall back on their institutional experience and culture when training with their Afghan counterparts. A doctrinal requirement of the training program is to improve the "professionalism" of the local national forces (Department of the Army 2006a, Table 6-2). FM 3-24 defines host nation professionalism as follows:

Professional:

1. Security forces that are honest, impartial, and committed to protecting and serving the entire population, operating under the rule of law, and respecting human rights.

2. Security forces that are loyal to the central government and serving national interests, recognizing their role as the people's servants and not their masters" (Department of the Army 2006a, Table 5-3).

This description sounds like it could easily be applied to the US Army. Field Manual (FM) 1, *The Army*, describes the United States Army's professionalism: "Throughout its history, the Army has demonstrated respect for enduring principles and institutional characteristics in its service to the Nation. Among the first are the primacy of

3

the Constitution, the rule of law, and military subordination to civilian authority" (Department of the Army 2005, 1-34).

The similarity in definitions of professionalism between FM 3-24, *Counterinsurgency* and FM 1, *The Army* implies that US trainers will inherently attempt to transfer their model of professionalism onto their Afghan partners. It may take some time before the ANA can be expected to match American definitions of professionalism.

Is it even in an Afghan Kandak's (battalion) best interest to adopt a US professional model and activity patterns given the specifically local nature of the war in which they are engaged? FM 3-24 is less specific in this regard, simply stating that the Host Nation Security Forces should be "tactically proficient" (Department of the Army 2006a, Table 5-3). How would US soldiers measure that proficiency? Currently the U.S. Army uses using Standard Army Training System (SATS) metrics. Would the ANA measure themselves with the same system? It remains to be seen whether this is a practical goal that can be realized under reasonable time and resource restraints.

US training teams must keep in mind that the Afghan martial culture is unusually successful in resisting outside invasions (Wegener 2007). The British fought three wars, seized Kabul twice, retreated twice, and never managed to bring Afghanistan fully under their control. The Soviets invaded in order to salvage a collapsing client state, fought nine years, holding Kabul the entire time, retreated, and watched their client government fall three years later. If the United States truly wants to enable the ANSF to be capable of defending their independence, then they may want to be careful not to erase the Afghan's martial advantages by "helping" them build a cardboard copy of a western army.

4

This study predicted that among the areas of difficulty would be the technological approach that the US generally applies to many problems. Another area of difficulty is the level of discipline that is assumed in the US military but relatively hard to accomplish in developing nations. United States forces do not have to work under the assumption that their battalions will be under strength due to absenteeism. US commanders also naturally delegate a great deal of authority to junior leaders precisely because they trust them to follow commander's intent. The existence of loyal subordinates who exercise tactical initiative cannot always be assumed in the Afghan Army. US military forces value a tradition of service under civilian leaders. The same relationship between civilian government and military force does not exist in Afghanistan.

The next chapter will consist of a literature review which will describe the significance of the sources primarily used in this study. The literature review is a guideline for further research on this topic. It consists of a list of the most relevant works used in this thesis and their contributions to understanding Afghan and American martial culture.

CHAPTER 2

LITERATURE REVIEW

This study makes extensive use of historical accounts of both Afghan and US fighters, both by national and international observers. There was difficulty in finding Afghan native literature on its own wars. The lack of available literature may be due to the long periods of isolation the nation has experienced. A body of professional and official literature may exist based on comments made by Ali Jalali in some of his works (A. A. Jalali 2002).[2] However, recovering this work and making it accessible to an English reading audience is beyond the scope of this thesis. Most likely that project would begin in Kabul. Since there is insufficient work available, this study has been forced to rely heavily on the foreign observers, as well as primary source interviews with CGSC students with Afghanistan experience. The body of literature by and about US soldiers is overwhelming, and this study has used personal judgment to narrow the field to a usable sample.

This chapter is divided into five sections, each dealing with a critical area knowledge required to answer the primary and secondary questions. The literature on Afghanistan historical fighting methods is divided into three periods, Anglo-Afghan, Soviet-Afghan, Taliban and Operation Enduring Freedom. Each period is distinguished by the presence of a distinct foreign intervention that presents a unique threat and opportunity to the Afghan warrior. The fourth chapter describes other studies of Afghan

---

[2]Ali Jalali makes extensive references to Afghanistan's historical civil military relations. As a former officer in the Afghan Army and instructor at the Afghan Academy, Mr. Jalali is extremely well versed in his organizational history, and frequently refers to it in many of his writings.

warfare and the development of the ANA that is used to focus research. The final section deals with literature that defines and described US Military Culture and its development.

There is a great deal of primary resources from recent veterans of training teams. These are rich in anecdotal material but are not comprehensive comparisons. These are single data points of a larger picture. There is also a great deal of comparative descriptive literature about Afghan (usually Pashtun) social customs compared to American and European. These are useful in understanding the base cultures that this study is attempting to merge in the ANA, but they rarely describe the specific elements of the martial class in either culture.

Anglo-Afghan Period

The Anglo Afghan wars were the first large scale conflict between the modern west and Afghanistan. The three distinct Anglo-Afghan Wars were interspaced with almost constant skirmishes and raiding by Pashtun tribesmen along the North West Frontier and the Khyber Pass. Many of the myths about Afghan fighting capability originated in stories carried back by British soldiers serving in India. The oldest work used in this thesis is Lady Sale's *Journal of the First Afghan War*. As a senior military spouse, Lady Sale was sufficiently familiar with the military profession to provide a credible witness to the humiliating destruction of the British Kabul garrison as it attempted to retreat to Jellalabad in depth of winter 1842. She was able to record her own eyewitness accounts of the siege of Kabul from her roof, as well as secondhand stories from officers of her immediate acquaintance. Lady Sale records the siege and subsequent abandonment of the cantonment, and the first days of the march to Jellalabad. She was taken into captivity by the commander of the Afghan rebellion, Sirdar (prince) Akbar

Khan. The narrative is then split between Lady Sale's account of her months in captivity and the end of the retreat, described by Dr. Brydon. Dr. Brydon was the sole survivor of the retreat not to be captured by the Afghans (Sale 1969, 3-5).

Some aspects of Afghan warfare are immediately apparent in these accounts. The Afghan resistance is fractious and disorganized, creating considerable confusion to the British Political officers, and is probably the main reason that the commanders of the cantonment failed to quickly realize the magnitude of the danger to their garrison (Sale 1969, 10-12). The Afghan riflemen evidently outshoot the British regulars and Indian Sepoys with their jezails.[3] Afghans utilize unorthodox tactics on the battlefield, and negotiations and deceit are used to dumbfound, delay, and confuse the British. The "magnet effect" is described as local tribesmen appear at odd moments to join the running battle as it enters their territory. Conversely, these same tribesmen appear to have not been in direct command and control by the Sirdar (Sale 1969, 113-115).

The British returned to Afghanistan in 1878 in the Second Anglo-Afghan War. Once again the British found out that Afghanistan was much easier to invade than it was to conquer or even depart safely. The central Afghan Army virtually ceased to exist as the British advanced to Kabul. However, rebellion against British rule rose once again, this time centered in Herat. The British were concerned about their logistic difficulties, raiding tribesmen, and the dangerously thin deployment of their forces. They were not particularly worried about engaging the Afghans in pitched battle, based on their earlier

---

[3]Lady Florentia Sale, *A Journal of the First Afghan War* (Oxford: Oxford University Press 1969), 48. The jezail was a locally produced Afghan firearm, muzzle loading, with a long barrel and heavy bullet. It was fired on a rest stand for greater accuracy. Lady Sale credits particularly skilled jezailchees with effective fire at 300 yards.

experience. In the course of the campaign, the British developed an arrogant sloppiness in operating against the Afghans, which cost them dearly in Maiwand.[4]

Michael Grisson's MMAS Thesis describes the tactical reasons for this embarrassing defeat of British arms in "Teutoberg Forest, Little Bighorn, and Maiwand, why superior military force sometimes fails." Grisson's analysis breaks down the Afghan advantage in this battle. The Afghans possessed superior artillery from the Herat Garrison, a remnant of the central army, allied with tribal forces and religious fanatics called Ghazis (Grissom 2009, 91). The Afghans were socially unified in the face of an outside invasion, and the tribal contingent, most likely Pashtun, was homogenous. The Afghans had a superior moral cause in defending their homeland, in addition to religious fervor sparked by the cause of defending Islam. The British deployed an exhausted, outgunned force of mixed British regular and Indian Sepoys in open terrain that allowed the Afghan gunners a free field of fire. They may have expected that their superior concentration of rifle fire would break the Afghan masses. In this occasion it did not, but the Afghan artillery fire broke the sepoys, which caused the regulars to fall back in considerable disorder. Conventional history has half of the 66th Foot manfully fighting to the last man, and also focuses on the heroics of the horse artillery units withdrawing under intense pressure. Kipling's poem *That Day* suggests that the 66th panicked after taking some casualties from artillery fire and that their disorder resulted in chaotic hand

---

[4]Michael T. Grissom, "Teutoburg Forest, Little Bighorn, and Maiwand: Why Superior Forces Sometimes Fail" (Master's thesis, Command and General Staff College, Ft. Leavenworth, KS., 2009), 96-97. The British forces under BG Burroughs deployed against a larger opponent on open terrain, applying firepower from a long distance in a static position. In addition, his soldiers, particularly the sepoys, were exhausted and hungry from a previous all night movement, and short of artillery ammunition

to hand battle, "But, Christ! along the line o' flight they cut us up like sheep, An' that was all we gained by doin' so." Kipling had an intimate familiarity with the British Indian Army immediately after the Second Anglo-Afghan War, and his account may reflect the reality of how razor edged the previously easy British victories may have been.[5] Once the regulars and sepoys lost their regimented cohesion, they became easy prey to numerically superior Afghans who had ample motivation to revenge their past defeats.

Soviet-Afghan War

There is a great body of literature on this war; including some very entertaining anecdotal accounts by journalists brave enough to travel as embeds to the mujahidin. However, this study benefits greatly from a professional military study taken from Soviet and Afghan personal experiences to truly understand how the Afghans were able to outlast and eventually expel the Soviet Army. In addition, Mohammed Yousaf's *The Battle for Afghanistan* provides a valuable counterpoint from the inside of the operational level planning of the campaign. This study also uses some particularly interesting studies of the Afghan resistance written by professional soldiers and scholars as a secondary resource.

The Bear Went Over the Mountain and *The Other Side of the Mountain* are particularly useful because they provide repeated examples of tactics used by both sides. In some cases it is apparent that ineffective tactics were adapted to changing situations, in

---

[5]Grissom, 89. Grissom explains that in previous battles Anglo Indian forces had withstood massed charges of Afghan infantry by forming company squares and maintaining disciplined fire.

other cases habits develop either due to stubbornness or the lack of the enemy to adapt. One example is the tendency of the mujahidin to use the same ambush sites again and again, which may have been dictated by terrain. The Soviet-DRA convoys apparently never developed adequate counter ambush tactics, which allowed the mujahidin to get away with being predictable (Grau and Jalali 1996, 67-68).

The value in the three books listed above is that they provide three different points of view of the same battles. In *The Bear Went Over the Mountain*, the tactical account comes directly from the Frunze academy after action reports, with contextual analysis by Lester Grau. In *The Other Side of the Mountain*, the vignettes are written from interviews with former mujahidin commanders. Mohammad Yousaf provides a sympathetic professional outsider's view of the mujahidin in *The Battle For Afghanistan.* BG Yousaf was a professional infantry officer with no special operations training before he took over the Pakistani ISI (Inter-Services Intelligence) effort to supply the mujahidin and coordinate their efforts at an operational level (Yousaf and Adkin 1992, 1-3). BG Yousaf is a conventionally trained observer who closely observed mujahidin operations closely, and developed techniques to work within their specific martial culture. He provides a third point of view from a perspective that may be quite similar to that of our Embedded Training Teams today.

The short vignettes in *The Other Side of the Mountain* are useful for a cultural study because of what they say as well as what they do not. Many Afghan accounts of tactical movement sound as if the mujahidin casually strolled around the battlefield. This was not likely in most cases, they would not have survived to tell their stories if they had not exercised basic tactical discipline. It does indicate that movement was routine, and

11

that utilizing terrain to conceal movement was sufficiently standard practice as not to require special mention (Grau and Jalali 1996, 55-59).

The vignettes also describe the mujahidin logistical difficulties. In many ways, warfare in Afghanistan was a battle of logistics. The mujahidin's main threat to Soviet control of Afghanistan was their ability to periodically interdict land lines of communications (LLOCs) (Grau and Jalali 1996, 3). The Soviets countered by rendering much of the rural countryside uninhabitable with mines, indiscriminate bombing, and other reprisal actions. This removed the primary source of direct logistical support to local mujahidin groups. The supply routes across the Afghanistan-Pakistan border were mountainous and restricted primarily to foot and animal traffic. Ammunition, weapons, and other supplies were delivered at great effort and expense. While few commentators remark a great deal on tactical movement techniques by fighters, many discuss the time and effort required to preposition supplies for large operations, or lament the failure of a battle group's ability to press home an attack when they ran out of ammunition (Grau and Jalali 1996, 178-179).

BG Yousaf remarks that few of the journalist accounts of what he calls the "Jehad" were sufficiently accurate to be used as credible sources. One exception that he noted was Robert D. Kaplan's *Soldiers of God* (Yousaf and Adkin 1992). Kaplan was one of the few western journalists considered fit enough and trusted enough to embed with mujahidin battle groups in Afghanistan. Kaplan's stories were obtained at considerable risk to his own health from the extraordinarily rough life in the afghan field as well as from potential Soviet action. Kaplan provides an account of the conditions under which the mujahidin traveled from their safe areas in Pakistan to the combat zone and how they fought and operated on a daily basis. This is information that would be considered to routine for the mujahidin themselves to describe directly in *The Other Side of the Mountain*, but is valuable because it describes the mujahidin attitude towards moving, communicating, eating, and sleeping. As anyone with direct experience in a combat zone in any nation knows, these activities consume far more time in a combat soldier's life than actual shooting (Kaplan 1990, 90-105).

<u>The Taliban and Operation Enduring Freedom</u>

The rise of the Taliban and the development of the new Afghan National Army are categorized into a single category because these two items are fundamentally linked. The Taliban rose in response to the chaotic civil war that immediately followed the fall of Kabul to the mujahidin in 1992. While the Soviet Union remained a constant and threatening presence in the country, the Afghan resistance forces managed to share the field with limited conflict. Once the outside pressure of the invader was removed, the various mujahidin resistance parties began to compete with each other for control of the post government. The final collapse of central order in 1992 led to a period of warlordism that Afghanistan has still not fully recovered from (Rashid 2000, 21).

The first response to the warlords was the Taliban. The Taliban were madrassa students who rose up against warlord depredations in late 1994, and subsequently gained full Pakistani patronage in their sweep outwards. The Taliban swarmed over Jellalabad, Heart, Mazar-E-Sharif, and Kabul. Only the area around the Panshir valley remained free of Taliban control, defended by a conglomeration of former mujahidin led by Ahmad Shah Massoud and his Tajiks. Pakistani reporter Ahmed Rashid describes the Taliban and

13

their rise to power in *Taliban*. Rashid had a level of access that western reporters lacked to Taliban areas and interviewed Taliban leadership (Rashid 2000, ix).

According to Rashid, what the Taliban lacked in military skill, they made up for in religious fervor, discipline, and political skill in bribing the enemy out of their way. More skilled and experience mujahidin leaders such as Ismael Khan, Rashid Dostum, and Ahmad Shah Massoud repeatedly beat back Taliban assaults. Mullah Omars' militia was blessed with substantial Pakistani and Saudi financial support. The Taliban also benefitted from substantial war weariness in the greater Afghan population. His primary war machine was the Toyota pickup truck. The maneuver was the mass swarm. Gradually the Taliban gained some organizational tactical skill as they absorbed mujahidin and militia battle groups. However, the irregular influx of new and inexperienced Taliban from the religious schools diluted this expertise, and the senior leaders remained distrustful of new recruits that they did not know personally (Rashid 2000, 98).

John Lee Anderson travelled to the Northern Alliance stronghold in the Panshir Valley in fall of 2001 in order to report on the advance against Taliban lines. He observed the relative lack of discipline in the alliance mujahidin fighters, as opposed to the discipline demonstrated by the Taliban. Anderson also directly witnessed a small example of what has become a regular feature of Afghan civil war, the ability of fighting groups to change sides as the situation dictates with little obvious loss of credibility or respect. This is a feature of true warlordism, as it demonstrates that even small unit military leaders act as political entities unto themselves. Anderson also described the growing cult of worship around the late Massoud, assassinated two days before 9/11 (Anderson 2002, 5).

The initial US invasion of Afghanistan relied heavily on local forces, such as the Northern Alliance and southern Pashtun Durrani tribes. Sean Naylor has put together a graphic account of an early attempt by US Special Forces (SF) to use a homegrown militia as a maneuver force in *Not a Good Day to Die*, the story of Operation Anaconda. This brutal battle was primarily fought between US soldiers and Al Qaeda, but the main effort was originally intended to be the SF led militia force. The Afghans failed in their mission, partially because the Americans did not properly coordinate their support, and partially because the Americans did not sufficiently understand the internal dynamics of the militia force, and its organizational weaknesses (Naylor 2005, 214-215).

There is an interesting dynamic about Operation Anaconda that has in some ways repeated itself in other areas of the country up to the present day. While the Al Qaeda forces fight tenaciously and in many cases skillfully, the Afghan militia required significant effort to get organized. The SF soldiers discovered that the tactical skill of the Afghans was pitifully low, many of the men having never seen combat. As the preparations for the mission progressed, the SF soldiers realized that at least one contingent had conflicted loyalties, which prompted them to rely increasingly on a smaller "elite" element. When engaged, the militia quickly lost cohesion. The disintegration was sped by the obvious lack of American firepower in response to al Qaeda's mortars and artillery (Naylor 2005, 276-279). The militia hastily beat a retreat out of range, and began to fight among themselves. The leader that the Americans had relied on had to be talked out of attacking a small village in the next valley out of frustration (Naylor 2005, 280). This difficulty of the US sponsored Afghan National

15

Army (ANA) to maintain cohesion in the face of an apparently unwavering enemy is still apparent today (Koning 2009, 5).

Other Research Studies

Professional studies are available that analyze various aspects of the current campaign in Afghanistan, including the nature of warlordism, the record of specific leaders such as Ismael Khan and Rashid Dostum, and the particular problem of building the ANA from scratch. There is currently a vigorous debate on the feasibility of continuing to develop a strong central army as opposed to institutionalizing a national tribal militia system. The tribal advocates, such as Major Jim Gant, believe that the ANA would never be strong enough to combat the Taliban (Gant 2009). ANA supporters argue that the only hope of national unity revolves around a strong national army and its representation of nationalism (Grau and Jalali 1996, 79).

Historically, Major Gant is correct. The Afghan central army in any of its forms was never capable of protecting the nation's sovereign integrity from outside invaders. In every modern case, the invaders have left after internal resistance has made their continued presence untenable. The internal resistance has frequently contained elements of the army, but is composed in greater numbers from local militia, and is usually not led by military officers (Grau and Jalali 1996). Gant's recommendation that tribal security forces be established and supported in combination with the current effort with the ANA and Afghan national Police (ANP) (Gant 2009). Gant's paper also has several useful observations about his Operational detachment Alpha (ODA) cooperation with a single tribe and the internal dynamics that led to his success. They will be referenced in the analysis and conclusions of this thesis.

16

The Australian Army's Lieutenant Andrew Wegener's *A Complex and Changing Dynamic* is a comprehensive study of the Afghan response to the British, Soviet, and US coalition interventions. Lieutenant Wegener describes these reactions as a complex political social function that reflected the cultural values and interests of a system of micro-societies rather than the purpose of the central state. He also discusses the enormous damage caused by the Taraki regime in 1978-79 to the traditional tribal elites, which was continued in even more violent form by the Soviet occupation (Wegener 2007, 54-55). The Soviet occupation further also fragmented and weakened the urban educated elite. The Taliban rule continued the weakening of the both educated and traditional leadership at the expense of religious authority figures. The traditional elite has been largely replaced by local warlords (Wegener 2007, 21-24), suggesting that Major Gant's success at establishing security through a local tribe may not be easily replicated throughout Afghanistan.

Thomas Barfield's "Weapons of the Not So Weak in Afghanistan" describes the relationship between the two primary Pashtun tribal groups, Durrani and Ghilzai. The Durranis, of whom which Hamid Karzai is the most famous to non Afghans, have traditionally been the rulers of Afghanistan between wars (Barfield 2007, 2). The Ghilzais, however, have more often been the primary movement to expel invaders in Afghanistan's history. Barfield explains that the more egalitarian tribal structure of the Ghilzai, concentrated in broken and mountainous land, makes the leadership of tribal groups more precarious, as it is based on personal influence and persuasion, rather than land ownership or familial position. Therefore the Ghilzais more often than not preferred to stay as close to home as possible in order to protect their personal power (Barfield

17

2007, 3-4). Durrani leaders relied more on ownership and management of large agricultural areas, which yielded a more concrete authority based on patronage that was more hierarchical and easily maintained in absentia. This meant that Durrani chiefs had not only the money but the time to politic in Kabul. Their political power in Helmand or Kandahar was much more secure than their Ghilzai rivals in the mountains. However, the Ghilzais were more hardened to risk and less vulnerable to outside pressure, making them more natural leaders in a time of national resistance than the Durranis, who had much more to lose to destabilization of the status quo.

Haydar Mili and Jason Townshend explain in "Tribal Dynamics of the Afghanistan and Pakistan Insurgencies" that lately the Ghilzai dominated Taliban are gradually being replaced at the low and mid level leadership by Durranis as the movement expand into traditional Durrani strongholds like Helmand, Kandahar, and Heart (Milli and Townshend 2009, 8). This demonstrates that the tribal confederations cannot be considered monolithic organizations led and controlled by a single leader. In practice the Durranis and Ghilzais can be broken down further into clans, sub clans, and family groups (TRADOC 2009, 6). Each element acts in its own interest.

Ali Ahmad Jalali argues that a strong national army is essential to stabilizing the nation in "Rebuilding the Afghan National Army." He admits that historically the central government has had considerable problem maintaining the state control on military power considered a key pillar of a sovereign state. He also admits that this would be an expensive and time consuming effort, given the development of a broad based and legitimate government, resources, and time (A. A. Jalali 2002). Since then the Karzai government is riddled with corruption and incompetence, and is accused of tampering

18

with national elections (Lafraie 2009, 107). A Center for Strategic and International Studies (CSIS) report indicates that the US has only recently begun to allocate sufficient financial resources, and the President Obama's recent speech indicates that time is running out (Cordesman 2009, 4).

In "Respectable Warlords? The Politics of State-Building in Post-Taleban Afghanistan," Dr. Antonio Giustozzi writes that the Jihad created a military class of Afghan, which naturally expects military power to confer political power and economic benefit. This is the root of Afghan warlordism that Dr. Giustozzi describes in his other papers. The leaders of this military class are likely to find transition to a civilian life difficult, and have resisted giving up their political autonomy to a Kabul government that they do not trust. Many of these warlords, such as Rashid Dostum, integrated into the Government of the Islamic Republic of Afghanistan (GIRoA) (Giustozzi 2003, 7-9).

Jeff Haynes believes that the ANA has shown some promise, and gives some examples of this in "Reforming the Afghan National Army," where a well led Afghan brigade planned and executed its own counterinsurgency mission with minimal outside help. Haynes stresses the value of competent leadership, and therefore is concerned that the proposed expansion of the ANA to 134,000 will dilute the already small pool of trained and effective staff officers and commanders. He recommends increasing the authorized size of the existing kandaks rather than generating whole new organizations. Haynes also criticizes the Capability Milestones (CM) currently in use as being too focused on resource management and not of operational effectiveness. The availability of equipment, men, and supplies does not automatically confer the ability or willingness to fight (Haynes 2009).

US Military Culture

Numerous studies have been written about the US Military. We like to read and write about ourselves. American military culture has developed over time, and has been influenced by our geographical position, conflicts, enemies, social, and political influences. Some studies used are critical, some are praising, and many agree on certain trends. For example, no study argues against the American Military's specific reliance and comfort with technology.

Russell Weigley describes in *The American Way of War* how the US gradually evolved towards favoring strategies of annihilation over strategies of attrition as the nation gained the strength to execute the former. Americans gained the strength to completely overthrow their enemies, which led them to disdain limited wars as wasteful. The problem of American strategy is how to achieve the total victory desired without paying a prohibitive cost. Weigley was writing immediately after the Vietnam War, and he ends his thesis by explaining how the expectation that war will have total goals and waged with total resources has foundered in the age of limited war since the conclusion of the World War II. At the end of the Vietnam War the US Military, particularly the Army, was disillusioned and confused after losing a war because the public had withdrawn their support (Weigley 1973, xxii).

Andrew Bacevich picks up the narrative and explains how after Vietnam the military institution has come to be the most well regarded of any US government institution by its own citizens. The success in Grenada, Panama, and Desert Shield/Desert Storm restored the military's reputation in the eyes of the American public. As a smaller proportion of US citizens had practical experience in the military, ignorance contributed to the awe that the civilian public developed for its military forces. As a result of its own success, the US Military became increasingly unable to prevent their usage in Operations Other Than War (OOTW) that by their very title reflected the disdain of the officer class for anything that smacked of political and social complications or restraints (Bacevich 2005).

As of this thesis, the volunteer military has been in place for 27 years. The military age population pool has no living memory of a military requirement for citizenship. Only a small portion of this population is willing and able to enlist for military service. The rest have a large degree of public respect for military service but are glad that they do not have to do it. Not used to civilian challenge, US Soldiers may take for granted that the civilian population will continue to trust them. Other countries' militaries, particularly ones with a fragmented and chaotic history such as Afghanistan, may not be able to expect anything approaching that level of respect and trust from the population.

Adrian Lewis describes the evolution of US military culture in *The American Culture of War*. He believes that much of this culture originated on the frontier. The current American way of war has developed in response to changing technologies and circumstances following World War II. Lewis described the traditional way of war as marked by its totality of effort and equality of sacrifice, which legitimized the mass drafts and total victory expectations of World War II. War is unlimited, to be fought with minimal political interference, which results from the American public's expectations that wars have to be won, as only absolute political objectives justify the United States going to war at all. The war should be brought to a victorious conclusion as soon as possible. A sustained war is bad for the nation as it hurts the people and jeopardizes liberty. Finally, the US relies on a small military in peacetime, and can call on the vast material strength of the US for a short duration in time of war (Lewis 2007, 22).

This way of warfare collapsed under the strain of the Vietnam War. The blind faith that Americans had formerly placed in their government in times of war was gone. The response was to develop a professionalized volunteer army that would be capable of fighting the Soviet Union on short notice without a mass draft. This would negate the politically painful decision to gain mass public approval for military action. The Army would maintain much of its combat power in the National Guard and Reserve, which would maintain a connection to the citizenry. All soldiers would now be volunteers, which removed the requirement of military service from citizenship. This eliminated the tenet of equality of sacrifice, and the old tradition that every American male was a potential rifleman (Lewis 2007, 34).

The modern war to be waged by the professional army was far too complicated to be learned by short term conscripts, and even the infantry branch was being technologized with the development of the infantry fighting vehicle and anti tank guided missiles. The increasing technical complexity of warfare, combined with the professionalization of all ranks, enabled the US to develop a military force that exceeded all others on earth in high intensity combat.

The Center for Strategic and International Studies commissioned a report on military morale at the turn of the century, titled *American Military Culture in the 21st Century*. This information is all prior to 9/11, but it forms a recent enough model of the institution that has been and will continue to stand up the new ANA. The working definition of military culture is that it "induces common expectations about acceptable behaviors and attitudes among those in uniform, particularly in times of stress and danger." I believe that this definition is sufficient for a study of any martial subculture.

The study identified the fundamental military values were defined as self sacrifice, discipline, obedience to lawful authority, and high standards of performance (to be measured repeatedly and infinitely). These values are directly linked to the US Constitution (The Center for Strategic and International Studies 2000, 7).

These values are reflected in how the US fits the four elements of military culture, defined as professional ethos, ceremony and etiquette, cohesion, and esprit de Corps. These elements can also be used to analyze different military cultures. For the US military, discipline is reflected in our enforced organizational structure, and our requirement for units to follow higher headquarters purpose. Our Professional Ethos is reflected in physical and moral courage, a willingness to sacrifice, meritocracy, loyalty and respect for comrades, obedience to lawful authority, and a deep and abiding respect for civilian control of the military. Ceremony and etiquette are symbols of common identity and concrete evidence of the organization's core values. US Soldiers demonstrate respect for comrades who have sacrificed their lives by symbolically setting an empty table at formal events. Cohesion and Esprit de Corps are best represented by the ethos of equality of sacrifice, which expects leaders to lead from the front, and share risks and hardships with their subordinates, even down to eating last in the chow line.

The study identified a few areas of concern based on surveys from service members. These included an over-aversion to casualties (The Center for Strategic and International Studies 2000, 21), which undermined the value of self sacrifice, a tendency

23

to favor technical solutions, reliance on technology, requiring the military to field the best of all possible systems. These tendencies created a leadership trend to micromanagement and risk aversion (The Center for Strategic and International Studies 2000, 23).

The next chapter will explain the research methodology used to compare Afghan and US martial culture. The methodology will provide a framework for feeding the information from the sources described in this chapter into a framework for common comparison.

CHAPTER 3

RESEARCH DESIGN

This chapter will define culture for the purposes of this study, particularly military or organizational subcultures. Then it will explain the methodology of the common framework of military subcultures. Finally it will explain how the available information will be distilled into the framework for the purpose of defining the Afghan martial subculture for comparison in chapter 4.

The primary research question is "What are the problem areas when merging two martial cultures when the US is training the Afghan National Army?" This study applied a very simple approach to answering this question. It develops a common model of military culture, defines it for both Afghanistan and the United States, then compares them to identify values and practices that match or contrast. These contrasts in cultural values suggest difficulties that will be faced when US Army and Marine Corps trainers develop the ANA.

It is important to understand what is being discussed when culture is being discussed in this study. FM 3-24, *Counterinsurgency* defines culture as 'A system of shared beliefs, values, customs, behaviors, and artifacts that members of a society use to cope with their world and with one another" (Department of the Army 2006a, 3-37). Hofstede described culture as software in a human computer, "Culture is the collective programming of the mind that distinguishes the members of 1 group or category of people from others" (Hofstede 2005, 4). Hofstede explains that this programming developed in layers accumulated with age and experience, beginning with the family, the larger community, and school and work.

While parent culture may determine military culture to a great extent most national cultures have developed a military subculture of some sort. The United States has a military culture. FM 1, *The Army* defines our military culture as a professional culture, "Each profession establishes a unique subculture that distinguishes practitioners from the society they serve while supporting and enhancing that society. Professions create their own standards of performance and codes of ethics to maintain their effectiveness. To that end, they develop particular vocabularies, establish journals, and sometimes adopt distinct forms of dress" (Department of the Army 2005, 1-40).

The research relies heavily on a center for Strategic and International Studies Report that evaluated and defined US Military culture in 2000. As base cultural values tend to change slowly or not at all, this study is relevant for the current time period (Hofstede 2005, 12-13). The study also provides a universal model of military culture that can be used as a common base of comparison. In the CSIS report, American Military Culture is described using a model designed by James Burke that comprises four essential elements of military culture:

1. Discipline: the ability to and method of regulating members

2. Professional Ethos: identity that defines the subculture from the parent and associated civilian cultures, sources of pride and authority

3. Ceremony and Etiquette: socially bonding activities, frequently overused but important to developing identity and representing professional values

4. Cohesion and Esprit de Corps: bond that hold fighting men together, source of their willingness to die for their cause (The Center for Strategic and International Studies 2000, 8).

Edgar Schein defined organizational culture as a 'pattern of shared basic assumptions that a group has learned as it solved its problems of external adaption and internal integration, that has worked well enough to be considered valid and therefore, to be taught to new members as the correct was to perceive, think, and feel in relation to these problems" (Pape 2009, 12). This pattern should be discernable from observation of the organization's actions and statements. Some of the shared assumptions and beliefs may be hidden.

Schein also structures organizational culture with three levels, artifacts, espoused beliefs, and underlying assumptions (Schein 1990). In the US Army, practices are artifacts because they are the observable evidence of the organizational culture. Espoused beliefs would be our doctrine and public values. The underlying assumptions may be identifiable from a study of the artifacts and espoused beliefs. For example, many studies identify a deep faith in technology solutions from observing our practice historically on relying on firepower and airpower to win battles, and our expectation that the US military will always have the best equipment and systems available (Bacevich 2005, 32).

Geert Hofstede also helps with his model of the cultural onion. The outer layer is formed by symbols, which are observables, words, gestures, or pictures that carry a meaning for that culture. The next layer is heroes, who are individuals who possess highly prized characteristics and serve as role models to other members of the culture. They are partially observable but specifics of what they are important may not be obvious to outsiders. The next layer is ritual, which are collective activities that may not serve a practical purpose, but are essential to social life. Practices cut across all three of the outside layers, they are observable to an outsider, but the cultural meaning may not be

27

discernable. The center of the onion is values, which are tendencies to prefer one state of affairs over another (Hofstede 2005, 7-8).

Hofstede's and Schein's models can be aligned side by side to develop an understanding of a martial subculture. The Schein's underlying assumptions are very similar in form and meaning to Hofstede's bedrock values. Schein's artifacts describe Hofstede's, rituals, heroes and practices. Hofstede could very well be describing Schein's espoused beliefs when he talks about rituals. Both theories of culture expect that a hidden core forms and effects all outside observable activity and social interaction. What this study has done is to reverse engineer the Afghan warrior Culture in order to identify some of the bedrock values.

While the exterior layers of organizational culture may change, the core values will most likely not. Values tend to remain relatively resistant to change (Hofstede 2005, 12-13). What will change are the practices in response to changes in environment. Symbols and heroes can change over time, particularly from generation to generation. An example of this would be the handshake, appropriate for adults, and a handclasp, appropriate for teenagers. Both symbols represent the same core value of respect in greeting, demonstrated through a physical contact. Observation of practices over time helps identify core values through identifying commonalities. Looking at practices at a snapshot in time may be deceptive. For example, for the Afghan warrior, the AK-47 does not have the same significance that a jezail had in the 19th century.[6]

---

[6]Sale, 48, 64; Chivers, *At War: Notes From the Front Line*. Lady Sale describes two snipers, known by name, who were capable of shooting sentries through loopholes in the Kabul garrison in 1841. She opines that Afghan marksmen own their own weapons and have to supply their own powder and shot, and frugality leads to careful and accurate

Organizational culture is a sub culture of its parent cultures. National culture is the broadest, common to the largest group of people. Under that the possible layers can include regional, generational, class, and organizational subcultures (Hofstede 2005, 11). The various subcultures are not necessarily hierarchic and may interact laterally. For example, an organizational subculture may include or be influenced by class, generational, or gender culture. Organizational culture is not isolated from the parent and associated cultures. Therefore the Afghan martial culture is a reflection of Afghan national culture. It may have some aspects that represent Pashtun and Tajik ethnic cultures. There are some differences in how the mujahidin fought the Soviets in the 1980s, and how the Taliban fought their civil war in the 1990s, which is a generational culture difference because the majority of the Taliban grew up during the war, frequently in refugee camps as opposed to traditional villages (Rashid 2000, 89-90; Afsar and Samples 2008, 20-21). Afghan martial subculture can be understood within the context of national, ethnic, and tribal cultures.

In order to observe Afghan martial cultural practices over time, this study includes Afghanistan's military history since the first British invasion in 1838. The historical record clearly identifies preferred and successful methods of combat for Afghans. Organizational descriptions are useful as they explain how Afghans grouped for combat, and who tended to do most of the fighting. Accounts from Afghans, their enemy, and neutral observers tend to agree on the type of weapons used, and how this was partly

---

shooting. In contrast, C. J. Chivers analyzes the accuracy record and captured equipment in Marjah in early 2010, and opines that the prevalence of low quality AK-47s and poor quality ammunition has led to Afghan fighters who rely on large amounts of automatic fire rather than accuracy.

29

by choice and partly by necessity. The battle accounts describe Afghan activity under fire, what kinds of risk they were willing to take, and how they issued orders and maintained discipline. First person accounts reveal what elements are emphasized, and what individual actions on the battlefield deserve special mention. The historical research also illuminates Afghan motivation to fight, and what provided them with their staying power in the protracted wars that they have fought.

Using these observations, all through primary resources and secondary studies presented a problem, because the majority of these sources are from foreigners. There are few sources that are directly or immediately derived from an Afghan participant. This is probably due to the 28 percent literacy rate among combatants from the soviet war through the present day (Younossi et al. 2009, 3). They speak through the soldiers and journalists who are telling their story. So there is a filter, and this study attempts to account for that by utilizing multiple sources over time, and focusing on broad trend lines that are corroborated by different observations.

For example, Kaplan makes many references to Kipling while writing in Peshawar in the 1980s (Kaplan 1990, 9). However, quoting Kipling out of context will not explain the mujahidin's actions today. Kipling was a keen observer of the effect of the Afghans on the British soldiers he was familiar with, but he had no practical experience of fighting them. His first combat experience came long after, during the Boer war. However, it is possible that many western observers were looking to recreate Kiplinesque drama when they looked at the mujahidin. In other cases, both Pakistanis and

Americans tend to optimistically evaluate their success in training Afghans.[7] This optimism may be built on an expectation that a sample of Afghans trained directly by foreign forces will transmit these skills directly to their peers and subordinates.

Using a wide variety of these sources, this thesis developed a sketch of Afghan martial culture that has remained relatively stable over the last 160 years. Based on the cultural theories described above, the underlying values of Afghanistan's martial culture developed are enduring, and a successful ANA will be built around them, not the other way around. Coping strategies for overcoming conflicts in these values can only be proven in the field, and much relies on considerable human relations skill on both parties, and a willingness to change some practices in accordance with core values. It would be a mistake for an outside agent to attempt to change the core values of the Afghan culture against their will. Afghanistan's history of suggests that enforced cultural change will quickly be met with violent resistance.

The next chapter will define Afghan martial culture using the four essential elements of military culture, discipline, professional ethos, ceremony and etiquette, and cohesion. It will then compare this definition to the existing model of US military culture from the CSIS study of 2000, and describe the area of primary contrast.

---

[7]Brigadier General Yousaf proudly claims that his mujahidin developed better combat skills in training camps than the Pakistani Army regulars. He also claims that US observers were surprised to hear that mujahidin Stinger gunners had better than predicted success.

CHAPTER 4

ANALYSIS

Afghan martial culture: Afghan martial culture is traditionally that of a tribal militia. It is oriented on armed members of tribal and local communities outside of the large cities, in rural regions where most of the population lives. In Afghanistan, this militia, or lashkar, is responsible for defending the tribe's interests against incursion from interlopers, whether they are other tribes, the Kabul government, or a foreign army. The lashkar has demonstrated the historical capability to band together and coordinate active defense against Afghanistan's foreign enemies when the central government army has failed. The lashkar does not normally form an organized fighting unit, but is a loose conglomeration of smaller battle groups oriented around family or village identity.

Leadership in the lashkar is based on personal example, power of persuasion, and ability to provide resources. It is challengeable by other members of the battle group. The lashkar highly values personal skill in its members. Historically the valued skills have included marksmanship and horsemanship in particular, but modern battlefield conditions have caused the valued skill set to become more technical in nature, with explosive skills in particular being valued (Grau and Jalali 1996, 141). The lashkar is loyal first to its primary identity group, which is based on qawm and familial ties. Lashkar battle groups can split from the main body when and if circumstances change or a greater threat is presented to their home territory (Grau and Jalali 1996, 170). They are most comfortable fighting at home, where they know the terrain and population and can count on resupply (Grau and Jalali 1996, 169).

Based on Afghanistan's military history, the lashkar is the successful military model, and the identity that most Afghans will naturally identify with. The mujahedeen have a romantic identity as the simple defenders of their homeland that government forces will have a hard time matching. Successful Afghan central military operations have included most or some of the lashkar's elements. An example of this merging is the large number of tribal militia and ghazis (religious fanatics) at the Battle of Maiwand used to flesh out the core of regulars from Kandahar and Herat (Grissom 2009, 90). Another example is the relatively successful use of tribal militia by the Democratic Republic of Afghanistan (DRA) to interdict mujahidin supply across the Pakistan border, extending government power in area that the regular army could not survive (Kaplan 1990, 99-100). An even more recent example is the battlefield success of US soldiers such as MAJ Gant in countering Taliban and Al Qaeda forces by co-opting local tribal forces (Gant 2009, 15-22).

The characteristics of the lashkar and Afghan warriors can be generically described using James Burk's model of military culture, using four categories: discipline, professional ethos, ceremony and etiquette, and cohesion/esprit de corps. And evaluation of these four characteristics can help identify core values in the Afghan martial traditions (The Center for Strategic and International Studies 2000, 8).

Discipline: Leaders exercise discipline through personal influence with the members of their battle groups (TRADOC 2009, 13). This tie will be strong or weak based on the power of that influence, and can change according to the fortunes of the battlefield and personal relationships. When combined into larger groups, even when cooperating with regular military units, the individual battle groups have considered themselves politically independent units that can enter or depart the battle at will.[8] This was demonstrated numerous times during the Soviet war when groups of mujahidin left battles when conditions changed to their detriment, or their home territory was threatened (Grau and Jalali 1996, 170). This habit frequently exposed other battle groups to increased danger when flanks or lines of communication (LOCs) were exposed, but is commented on matter of factly by the mujahidin themselves. This reveals that this kind of activity on the battlefield was known, and understood, if not appreciated.

Another characteristic is the "magnetic" attraction of fighters to a battle in their area. This was recorded as early as the 1842 retreat from Kabul (Sale 1969, 121), and described frequently in the soviet war (Grau and Jalali 1996, 162), and even in the 2001 US led eviction of the Taliban (Anderson 2002). This attraction is naturally stronger the bigger or more successful a battle may appear to be, and can provide needed numbers of combatants to the Afghan side. It can also present command and control difficulties when unknown leaders suddenly appear to take their share of the victory and loot.

Individual manpower levels are constantly fluctuating as fighters are needed elsewhere to attend to personal matters. These can be as mundane as tending a field during harvest time. Lashkar fighters are normally unpaid, and have to provide for their families in addition to fighting (Grau and Jalali 1996, 22). Even when paid a regular wage, such as in the ANA, absenteeism is a significant problem, sometimes simply because a soldier must hand carry cash to a distant family, due to a lack of trustworthy money transfer systems (Koning 2009, 7). Mujahidin leaders openly admitted to the

---

[8]Retirement is considered honorable as long as it is a group activity (Barfield 2007). The operational problem for Afghan forces is that group identities are small, and usually do not encompass the entire engaged force. "It's those guys problem now."

Pakistanis that they could normally field no more than third of their battle group's strength on short notice, and that it would take considerable time and coordination to muster a majority of the potential fighting strength for special operations (Yousaf and Adkin 1992, 34).

The Taliban was frequently noted for being frequently well disciplined compared to the mujahidin forces that they fought. This has to be understood in context of who and what they are (Anderson 2002, 88). The Taliban is identified by a specific religious fanatic identity. This belief in one version of Islam has been uniformly indoctrinated in madrassas located in Afghanistan and Pakistan. The religious education is marked by a preference for rote memorization of Koranic verses in original Arabic, as opposed to a deep discussion and debate of spiritual issues. Many of these students are refugees, displaced from the normal village life, where the traditional male role models were frequently absent fighting the Soviets. This second generation of mujahidin had a relatively shallow identity, and was therefore quite amenable to being used as religious shock troops (Rashid 2000). They did not question their subordinate role because they had no experience outside the religious school. This condition does not last long. By 2001, Taliban battle groups were deserting under their commanders to the Northern Alliance when they saw the opportunity (Anderson 2002, 80-87).

The DRA military was designed on a Soviet model, which was particularly ill suited to civil war in Afghanistan (Grau 2005). The soviet battle command methodology was strictly authoritarian and hierarchical. It left very little decision making authority to junior leaders on the front lines, and tightly controlled resources from high headquarters, both to ensure loyalty and control black market sales to the enemy. The DRA that resulted was ill trained and equipped at the platoon level, and a predictable and unimaginative opponent for the mujahidin. After the collapse of the Soviet Unions, the DRA military fragmented into warlord elements either under their own commanders, such as Rashid Dostum, or melded into mujahidin factions. Officers and soldiers in the ANA who served with the DRA Army tend to retain a preference for Soviet style command and control (Koning 2009, 5).

Professional Ethos: The tribal warrior exists to secure tribal internal interests and defend against outside intrusion. In this context the "tribe" may be a qawm or other community, or even an ethnic organization, such as the Uzbek Junbesh (Giustozzi 2003). Fighting is one method of settling the numerous conflicts that develop between the micro societies that dot Afghanistan. Fighting, or more accurately killing, is a path to proving manhood, and worth to the community as a defender. Some researchers contest that Afghanistan can accurately be called "tribal":

> Anthropologists and historians who study Afghanistan don't use "tribe" as an analytical unit. Instead, they talk about a word that is often translated as "tribe," but has a lot of other meanings as well. That word is *qawm*. The best translation for *qawm* is "solidarity group," meaning a group of people that acts as a single unit and is organized on the basis of some shared identity. (TRADOC 2009, 8)

Afghan warriors have no problem historically sacrificing their lives in battle. Even in their historical victories they have most likely lost more lives on the battlefield than their opponents. In killing more than 13,000 Soviets, 1.3 million Afghans died (Feifer 2009, 255) over ten years. In looking back at the Soviet expulsion with pride, the Afghans demonstrate that they have great willingness to sacrifice their lives. Afghans have consistently demonstrated conspicuous bravery on their battlefields. This bravery is fueled occasionally by religious certitude that they are defending their religion, and always by pride (TRADOC 2009, 12).

While Afghans can demonstrate bravery that may appear foolhardy to casualty averse westerners, they are not, and never have been, suicidal (Yousaf and Adkin 1992, 31). One of the critical tactical skills of the Afghan warrior has been to know how and when to run away. Unlike the Japanese Bushido culture, which found retreat so distasteful as to restrict tactical options, the Afghan warrior is free to retire from the battlefield if he feels that the objective is not worth the sacrifice. Afghans retreated in the face of superior combat power, whether it was Soviet, British, American, or even Afghan. There is more glory in close combat than in passively submitting to bombardment (Yousaf and Adkin 1992, 36). This marks a departure from the western tradition of standing fast in the face of fire.

Afghans generally intend to be on the sending side of the fire. Here it is useful to explain the changing nature of skills the Afghan warrior values. Individual skill has always been highly valued. In Kipling's day, the Afghan frontier evidently boasted some very effective snipers. Lady Sale notes that Afghan jezailchees outshoot the British and Indian musketeers, and even manages to hear about two particularly good snipers in particular (Sale 1969, 48). Marksmanship was evidently highly valued in traditional Afghan warfare. This is not surprising. The Afghans had a domestic weapon industry that made practical Martini-Henry copies well into the 20th century (Thomas 1925, 34). The ability to kill a man at long range is obviously valuable for feuding clans in mountainous areas. From reading between the lines of Lady Sale's accounts it appears that either accurate jezails or accurate Afghans were in short supply. If every Afghan was able to pick off a sentry through a loophole in the cantonment the army would never have survived to begin their retreat. As it was, the Afghans took a leisurely (or tortuously) seven days to finish off the British Army, which consisted of less than 5,000 hungry and frozen combatants and more than 12,000 camp followers- hardly an overwhelming force (Sale 1969, 95). It appears that there were a few good shots that made their appearance on the battlefield very painful for the British, while the majority of Afghans waited until the British elements were sufficiently weakened in order to be engaged with close combat. As late as the battles of 1878, Grissom remarks that large proportions of Afghan irregular infantry were armed exclusively with swords (Grissom 2009, 95).

By the 1980s the common weapon of the Afghan became the AK-47, which is hardly a precision weapon. As the author has learned from personal experience, the AK-47 is a tricky rifle to zero, a difficulty compounded when equipped with a wide variety of manufacturing tolerances. The mujahidin were good enough shots to fight the Soviets and DRA, similarly equipped. However, the mujahidin regularly recount the continued use of "five shooters" and "ten shooters," or Mosin-Nagant and Lee-Enfield rifles respectively. The Lee-Enfields[9] are mentioned for their long range and ability to pierce Soviet body armor (Grau and Jalali 1996, 244), which indicates that fighters with these weapons could not have been low skilled. Chivers points out that the Lee-Enfield is still present on the

---

[9]The Martini-Henry was the main British battle rifle of the 2nd Angle Afghan war, and fired a single .45 caliber bullet (Grissom 2009). The Mosin-Nagant M1891 was the main Russian battle rifle in the early 20th century, and fired five 7.62x54mm bullets (five shooter). The Lee-Enfield was the standard British battle rifle of the early 20th century and fires ten .303 caliber bullets (ten shooter) (Grau and Jalali; author's collection).

battlefield today, and his commentary is accompanied by video of a US marine squad pinned down by a single rifleman (Chivers, At War: Notes From the Front Line 2010).

Currently, the Taliban is renowned for their low marksmanship skills (Chivers, At War: Notes From the Front Line 2010). What happened? This study suggests that the answer lies in the shift in priorities. In 1842, and again in 1880, the rifle was the weapon most useful for the lashkar fighter. By the Soviet war, fighting opponents equipped with armored vehicles, long range artillery, and helicopters, rifle marksmanship was important but not decisive. The mujahidin accounts tend to mention individuals by name that made particular contributions in the battle group. They are frequently mentioned for bravery, tactical judgment, and skill with explosives. Later, skilled individuals are entrusted with Stinger missiles that have a proven ability to use them at the right time correctly (Yousaf and Adkin 1992, 176). In contrast, the AK-47 can be fired by virtually anyone.

The Taliban has more success on attacking ISAF forces through explosives than through rifle fire. There are five coalition casualties from explosives for every single gunshot wound (Defence Manpower Data Center 2010). That does not mean that marksmanship is not important. It means that with a limited number of men who can see clearly, shoot well, and intelligently pick targets, the Afghans have pragmatically reinforced success, and pushed their resources and talent in the direction of explosives.

Afghan qawm battle groups are as autonomous as the micro-communities that they represent. The tradition tends to place great autonomy on the battle group commanders, and they exercise that freedom at their discretion. This characteristic is responsible for the remarkable ability of Afghans to change sides in war.[10]The Taliban utilized their Pakistani and Saudi cash to entice large portions of their mujahidin enemies to defect to their side, which in effect gave them a financial fire support on the battlefield. [11]When the US led coalition appeared over the skies in 2001, many of the same battle group leaders changed sides back to the Northern Alliance, apparently without shame or penalty (Anderson 2002).

Rashid Dostum is perhaps one of the most successful examples of this ability cross battle lines. Dostum began his career in the pay of the DRA, and built his mini empire around Mazar-E-Sharif. Sensing that the Najibullah government was finally at the end of its tether, he sided with Ahmad Shah Massoud, facilitating the mujahidin takeover of Kabul. Dostum initially sided with Massoud and Ismael Khan against the resurgent Taliban, only to betray them for a tactical advantage. When the Taliban ultimately took Mazar-E-Sharif, Dostum hid out in Turkey, only to return in 2001 on the side of the Northern Alliance, and eventually reestablished himself in his old territory. Since that time he has been a troublesome political personality for the Kabul government, and has been dismissed and recalled to office (Rashid 2000, 56-57).

Ceremony and Etiquette: The Afghans have very little outward signs of military ceremony. They have held military parades, when the central army was not too busy attempting to exert control over the countryside. Thomas observes one in 1923, but it

---

[10]Jon Lee Anderson, *The Lion's Grave* (New York, NY: Grove Press, 2002), 78. Abdullah Gar was a battle group leader who defected from Ahmad Shah Massoud to the Taliban and then back again, all according to Massoud's plan, or so he said.

[11]Ahmed Rashid, *Taliban* (New Haven: Yale University Press, 2000), 48. Haji Abdul Qadeer was convinced to hand over Jalalabad to the Taliban for $10 million.

appears that this was a relatively new convention based on western practice (Thomas 1925). The lashkar is loosely organized military unit, and rarely develops any recognizable ceremony. Etiquette is mostly the same that would be seen between traditional Afghans. A few practices seem to be common among lashkars that represent some of their values.

Public piety is recognized as a value as long as the individual is not too showy about it. Kaplan described his mujahidin as likely to pray whenever and wherever they felt the need to do so. They rarely, if ever, prayed in large groups or uniformly. It was never remarked on or discussed, much less proscribed. It was simply part of the individual battle rhythm to be handled on one's own time. When in the field, the practice of hard and uniform times of prayer appears to be relaxed to fit the conditions (Kaplan 1990, 124). The Taliban, by contrast, prayed in cohort, just as they had learned in madrassa.

Public justice also appears to be a habit of Afghan warriors, and for many of the same reasons as in western militaries. Dostum, Massoud, and the Taliban made regular use of public punishments for internal discipline (Giustozzi 2003, 8). In the mujahidin, and traditional tribal sense, this seems to be more a matter of demonstrating that the leader is capable of dispensing justice among his subordinates. Public justice is therefore a reassurance of the fairness of the leader, and can also be used as an object lesson to the other lashkar members. In extreme examples, particularly by Dostum and the Taliban, this method can lead to terrorizing subordinates.

This seems to be a good area to deal with the Afghan treatment of prisoners. According to Kipling, "When you're wounded and left on Afghanistan's plains, an' the women come out to cut up what remains, jest roll to your rifle and blow out your brains, an' go to your Gawd like a soldier."[12] This may have been an accurate depiction of anti-bandit operations in the mid 1880s on the Northwest frontier, but it has not always been the case with Afghan warfare. Afghans can, and have, taken prisoners. The Sirdar Akbar Khan took several British prisoners from the retreat to Jellalabad in 1842 (Sale 1969). Most of these prisoners were officers and their families, and the Sirdar probably intended to trade them for the safe return of his father, Dost Mahomed. The prisoners, including Lady Sale, were treated well, considering the circumstances. This is stark comparison to the treatment of the Indian portion of the army, which was slaughtered to a man along with their families (Sale 1969, 153).

Later, during the soviet war, the mujahidin took around 400 Soviet prisoners, though the fate of many was murky (Feifer 2009, 265). DRA soldiers were frequently taken prisoner, and absorbed into the mujahidin or released without their equipment (Grau and Jalali 1996, 92). Abdul Haq engineered the capture of Soviet General Akhrimiyuk from Kabul, but was dismayed when one of his subordinates killed him (Kaplan 1990, 160), primarily because the mujahidin had not yet capitalized on his kidnapping, but also because he felt sorry for the WWII veteran. Some of the Afghan and Pashtun tradition of hospitality can be extended, at least partially, to prisoners. However, the normal condition of the Afghan as the weaker party has limited their ability to hold prisoners. Afghans have also not generally attempted to take non western prisoners. Where they end up with them, it is occasionally by accident, and occasionally by intent.

---

[12]Kipling, The Young British Soldier

Many times prisoners are a hindrance to an insurgent force which can barely maintain and move itself.

The Taliban brutality towards captured Afghans was deviant enough to be remarked on, even though this was probably spurred in retaliation to Dostum's execution of Taliban prisoners.[13] The increasingly ethnic nature of Afghan warfare after the Taliban's entrance generated an increasing spiral of brutality that has left its mark on the Taliban's practices today (Lafraie 2009, 106). In the current operating environment, it would not be advisable for an ISAF soldier to fall into the hands of the Taliban.

Cohesion and Esprit de Corps: Afghan lashkar groups, warlords, and militia could be described as having no normal organizational cohesion whatsoever. This would be missing the value of the micro armies that emanate from the micro societies of Afghanistan (Wegener 2007). Each of these battle groups has the potential to develop into tightly knit units under inspiring and capable leadership. Inside the group, the fighters will probably know other members quite well, and are motivated to fight for each other, and contribute value to the group. This can even extend to a willingness literally do the dirty work, as in one mujahidin whose name is remembered solely because he piled camel dung on explosives, "God bless Matin's soul, he used to put the manure on the mines" (Grau and Jalali 1996, 143).

Tactical and operational control was loose, and orders are not so much obeyed as agreed to. This represents the traditional lack of formal structure to the lashkar, and the

---

[13]Rashid, 73-77. Hazara involvement in the massacre of several thousand Taliban prisoners probably lent justification to Taliban brutality in Mazar-E-Sharif and Bamiyan province in1998. Prior to the Taliban War interethnic and intersect violence in Afghanistan was rarely mentioned.

negotiated alliance nature of the larger formations (Grau and Jalali 1996, 155). Mujahidin conducting large operations against the Soviets late in the 1980s or against the DRA in the early 1980s were conducting coalition warfare every bit as frustrating and multifaceted as NATO operations in Kosovo in 1999. The mujahidin were constitutionally unable to maintain their cohesion once the Soviets departed. Even during the siege of Jellalabad, Hekmatyr and Massoud's forces began fighting each other (Yousaf and Adkin 1992, 231).

When fighting the Soviets or British, Afghans were able to cooperate, but their combined forces were not a unified army, but something that more resembles a feudal host. At their most professional, the mujahidin were able to form mobile groups that stayed in the field for long periods of time, and were better trained, skilled, and equipped than their local contemporaries. However the locally oriented groups far outnumbered professionals. Large mujahidin operations had to be negotiated months in advance, particularly if they involved forces from more than one of the seven primary Peshawar parties (Grau and Jalali 1996, 175). Frequently the lack of coordination and command and control led to tactical failure of the large operations.[14]

The major motivating factor to national unity has been the revulsion at an outside invader, reinforced by religion (Grissom 2009, 90). Once the invader has been repelled, sometimes even before he has fully left the borders, the Afghans have tended into battle over the post war order. This fighting prevented the existence of a post war order after the

---

[14]"There is no coordination. If the Mujahidin attack on one side and keep the government busy, the mujahidin on the other side are sleeping." Mohammed Yousaf and Mark Adkin, *The Battle for Afghanistan* (Yorkshire: Pen and Sword, 1992), 228.

collapse of the DRA in 1992 (Rashid 2000). Aside from that, tribal coalitions can form based on temporary expedience or mutual interest, but rarely as enduring alliances.

Afghans have a strong tradition of fighting, and sacrifice is appreciated for the good of the tribe or faith. Mujahidin appear to have been relatively light hearted, considering the depressing exchange ratio they faced against their Soviet and DRA enemies (Kaplan 1990, 92). The average fighter has demonstrated an unusual resilience to maintain struggle over a very long period of time. Evidence suggests that the population is tired of conflict (Neamatollah, Mazurana, and Stites 2009, 115), and even the hardened Taliban leadership may be feeling fatigue (Rashid 2010). Even if the war were to end decisively this year, however, the Afghan conflict is one of the longest in modern history, lasting 31 years to this date. The lashkar has, with its internal group dynamics, generated sufficient esprit de corps to maintain fighting spirit for multiple generations.

The DRA military, by contrast, had strict organizational discipline, as noted above, but held little cohesion on its own. The DRA drafted manpower for its army, and was never a popular career choice for Afghan males. The DRA habitually press ganged recruits as part of cordon and search operations with the Soviets (Grau and Jalali 1996, 241). The DRA itself held little legitimacy with the greater bulk of the population, and its army was seen as a tool of the foreigners. The comparison between the DRA soldier, dressed and equipped similarly as his Soviet comrade, who together shelled and bombed Afghan villages, and the mujahidin, dressed like a traditional tribesman, with a captured rifle and little ammunition, who desperately fought the atheist invader, could not have been starker. In addition, the DRA soldier was poorly trained and equipped, and frequently used as cannon fodder on missions that the Soviets would not do themselves. For example, DRA soldiers were used to man isolated outposts that were subject to frequent mujahidin attack and interdiction. The DRA survived in these outposts on desperation and artillery support, hunkered down behind mines that often prevented him from leaving (Grau and Jalali 1996, 95). It is no wonder that soldiers in this situation willingly deserted, with their weapons and equipment, in large numbers to the mujahidin. It was not uncommon for these same soldiers to use their military skills with much more vigor as unpaid volunteers in the resistance. The justice of their new cause made a great deal of difference. This is not to say that the DRA never fought well. They did, when paired with Soviet units or in situations where there was no obvious alternative. The DRA survived four years after the departure of Soviet combat soldiers on its own combat power. However this was due to mujahidin disunity and massive amounts of Soviet material and financial aid (Yousaf and Adkin 1992, 230-231). These were also defensive battles for large populated cities, such as Jellalabad and Kabul, where the DRA could set behind complex fortifications and use their superior firepower against the mujahidin.

Based on this model of the Afghan Warrior Culture, we can define some of the core values that Afghans hold as essential to their lashkar. Personal bravery, skill, willingness to sacrifice, tribal autonomy, and faith in the justice of their cause are all identifiable in the Afghan warrior ethos during its wars with outside forces and internally.

US Military Culture: US military culture is the result of more than two hundred years of history marked by a military obedience to civilian government. The military serves the political purpose of the elected representatives to the people of the United States, a role that is defined in the US Constitution (Department of the Army 2005). The

US fighting soldier traditionally has been highly individualistic, based on a role model of the frontier rifleman (Lewis 2007, 6). In this original ideal, every male citizen was theoretically capable of bearing arms in the militia to defend against incursions from outsiders, or to quell insurrection (Lewis 2007, 22). This ideal is still represented in the symbology of the Army National Guard. In some ways the colonial militia was not dissimilar from the lashkar of tribal Afghanistan. These were men who used their natural fighting skills to defend their communities with limited conventional military structure. They liked to do things "their way."

American soldiers have changed greatly since the origin of the colonial militia, and they have adopted many characteristics of western European warfare necessary to project power across the continent, and overseas. In many respects American military culture can be considered to be an offshoot of western military culture, with a specific US flavor (Hillen 1999, 2). This is the result of the unique American experiences in warfare, as well as the specific character of US political ideology. American military men and women have a history of being very loyal to their central government. In times of Civil War and popular unrest, the US Military has survived severe stress and maintained its status as a defender of government stability.

US Military forces have developed an exceptional ability to adopt new technologies in warfare, but have come to rely on this practice to such a great extent that critics have charged that the US fails to look beyond technical solutions to its military problems (The Center for Strategic and International Studies 2000, 8). This approach has also led to a belief that all matters of war can be quantified and measured, even intangibles such as the "hearts and minds" of Vietnam, Afghanistan, or Iraq. The mathematical and scientific approach frequently ignores the effect on the environment of softer human sciences, such as culture and relationships.

The US Military is highly organized, with set roles and responsibilities for each individual soldier complete with specified equipment for the job. The table of Organization and equipment can show an observer in nauseating detail exactly what equipment is authorized to accompany each section in a firing battery, and the specific number of people by job skills and authority to run that section. In addition, each item of equipment comes complete with its own list of organic parts and accessories that are required for the full usage of the item. Each soldier has specific tasks that he is expected to be proficient at, which are gradable, and adjust in difficulty as the soldier increases in rank (The Center for Strategic and International Studies 2000, xx). For the more complex collective tasks that incorporate tactics with technical performance, there are endless doctrine manuals, training plans, and handbooks.

This vast structure of organization may give the US military the appearance of robotic rigidity to an outside observer. Part of the benefit in the strict organization model is the ability to easily improvise within the unit, based on a thorough understanding of the fundamental purpose of the unit and its equipment, rather than a rote repetition of mechanical tasks. This is possible because the US military expects and generally get a high degree of technical ability in its recruits. Not only are recruits expected to be literate enough to read regulations and manuals, they are also expected to be capable of mastering basic software tools such as Windows, Outlook, and Share Portal. Junior soldiers are trained and required to repair complex machinery in the field, frequently without supervision of technical officers and senior NCOs. This is possible again because

48

many Americans citizens grow up tinkering with cars and trucks. The high level of technical competence combined with a high cultural preference for individuality allows US Soldiers to adjust and improvise within what would otherwise be a stultifying system.[15]

The Center for Strategic and International Studies defined American military culture using James Burk's four essential elements of military culture. They are discipline, professional ethos, ceremony and etiquette, and cohesion and esprit de corps. This study has adopted this definition with some additions from other US military cultural studies.

Discipline: Discipline separates a military force from an "armed mob" (The Center for Strategic and International Studies 2000, 8). The US military has traditionally high standards for its discipline. US discipline is defined as "Obedience that preserves initiative," as opposed to "demanding instant responses" (Department of the Army 2006B, 7-52-3). US discipline expects subordinates to accomplish the mission commander's mission, but allows latitude in exactly how, particularly as the situation changes. Discipline provides the purpose for armed force, as well as the boundaries for what is permissible and what is not. US forces are required to conduct painstaking Collateral Damage Estimates before striking targets in inhabited areas with bombs or artillery. This is a combination of technical capability and disciplined patience to ensure that civilians are endangered minimally in firefights.

---

[15]Geert Jan Hofstede, *Cultures and Organizations: Software of the Mind* (New York, NY: McGraw Hill. 2005), 74. The United States ranked number 1 out of 74 in Hofstede's study.

Discipline is enforced through the organizational structure of the military (The Center for Strategic and International Studies 2000, 8). Soldiers are supervised through a clear chain of command that leads to a Joint Force Commander. In between there are trained NCOs and Officers at specific levels of responsibility who have specific amounts of authority to enforce the discipline of their soldiers. Orders and regulations are expected to be followed, and noncompliance is punished through a graduated series of judicial and non judicial punishments that can be utilized at a commander's discretion.

Professional Ethos: The US military's professional ethos is centered on combat action (The Center for Strategic and International Studies 2000, 8). This is based on the traditional western way of war that expects decisive battle (Lewis 2007, 22). The US military trains for, even if it rarely practices, high intensity combat. This is its comfort zone. Particularly for the US Army, much of this orientation comes from the experience of World War II, reinforced with the post Cold War operations Just Cause and Desert Storm (Bacevich 2005).

The professional ethos demonstrates a willingness to fight and die for nation and unit. It includes physical and moral courage, and loyalty and respect for comrades. Much of this ethos rests on a value of equality of sacrifice (Lewis 2007, 22). Everyone is expected to share in the deprivations and danger of combat. This is demonstrated, symbolically, by commanders and 1st Sergeants eating only after they are sure that all of their soldiers have been fed. Some of these traditions come from democratic traditions of the volunteer militia. They help to maintain the continuity of the value of equality of sacrifice even though the US military is professional, and no longer expects equality of sacrifice from society at large (Lewis 2007, 34).

The professional Ethos of the American Military also includes a strong respect for civilian control of the military. This is enshrined in US law, and is a pillar of a stable democratic republic (The Center for Strategic and International Studies 2000, 7). The officer corps may advise the civilian government, but has no independent decision making power on national strategic issues. The US Navy may have preferred the majority of national effort to fight the Japanese after 1941, but the President of the United States sided with the Army that Nazi Germany would be the first effort. There was no question of the Navy independently refusing to support that decision.

Finally the US professional ethos rests on a tradition of meritocracy. This means that soldiers are promoted based on impartial standards of performance and potential (The Center for Strategic and International Studies 2000, xviii). Officers and NCOs are promoted by a board that theoretically looks at the records anonymously and grades them according to set criteria. The best qualified candidates are promoted. Nepotism, family privilege, and purchasing commissions are invalid criteria for advancement. This system demonstrates the value of professional competence.

Ceremony and Etiquette: Military ceremony is generally the outwards displays of the military culture's values. Professional militaries like the US have many ceremonies. Collectively they celebrate the unit or individual, and help develop a common identity, therefore assisting in the development of cohesion (The Center for Strategic and International Studies 2000, 8).

The tradition of a unit passing in review is a demonstration of the respect between the commander and soldiers, where values like equality of sacrifice and loyalty to comrades come into play. Even an act as simple as a weekly unit run has more ceremonial, team building purpose than physical training. A subordinate walks slightly to rear and left of his boss, symbolizing his loyalty to protect the weak flank.

Medals are symbolic in what they are given for. The US military demonstrates its high value on military life by awarding the highest medals for actions taken to save other's lives, frequently at the cost of one's own.[16] If medals were simply given for efficient killing, then bomber pilots would have most of them. The US Military has traditionally valued the lives of its members as US citizens much more highly than other national militaries.

Cohesion and Esprit de Corps: This is the measure of loyalty and bonding within the group, and pride and identification with the larger unit (The Center for Strategic and International Studies 2000, 9). The US military identifies itself by services, branches, and units, but this pride is not to the detriment of the military as a whole. The Army may be subdivided into functional branches, and then further into "cliques," such as Airborne or Ranger qualified personnel. These subdivisions at their extreme create subcultures that make interoperability difficult. This is particularly true after long periods of peacetime training when the various sub elements tend to stay "in house." In the first large US conducted operation of the Afghan war, "Anaconda" in 2002, the various US Special Forces, conventional infantry, and Air force personnel had considerable difficulty understanding and trusting each other (Naylor 2005).

---

[16]Department of the Army, Field Manual 1, *The Army* (Washington, DC: Headquarters, Department of the Army, 2005). Sergeant 1st Class Paul R. Smith, Master Sergeant Gary Gordon, Sergeant First Class Randall Shughart, three of the most recent Congressional Medal of Honor winner, were all awarded posthumously for sacrificing their lives in order to save comrades..

However sub group esprit de corps may make joint operations difficult, the overall cohesion of US military forces in relatively seamless from the perspective of most enemies. There is no opportunity to turn a US unit on the battlefield with pay or reward. US units of any service or branch will support one another in contact. A Theater Logistics Commander will not refuse to support the 101st Air Assault (AASLT) Division because he does not like that division's commander.

In combat, US soldiers display above average cohesion. Junior NCOs will immediately take over for wounded squad and platoon leaders, frustrating an enemy that successfully decapitated Soviet units (Department of the Army 2006b, 6-12). Based on their tradition of discipline that allows initiative, US Soldiers will continue to accomplish their mission even with key leaders disabled or dead, or if the primary route becomes impassable. US units under intense combat pressure rarely break apart and flee, mostly because to do so would be abandoning their comrades.[17]

Areas of conflict between US and Afghan martial cultures: The US and Afghan cultures have some military values in common. Among these are a loyalty to comrades, and willingness to sacrifice, and the equality of that sacrifice. Both cultures highly value and respect military skills and battlefield courage. Both cultures originate from a tradition of rugged individualism and have a shared military history of winning independence through violent resistance.

---

[17]Regina F. Titunik, "The Myth of the Macho Military," *Polity* (April). Titunik explains how the strong teamwork and comradeship in the military dilutes the stereotype of excessive machismo.

There are four areas where values will conflict or are defined in radically different ways. These areas are in the type of loyalty valued, the way skills are valued, attitude towards organization, and motivation for combat.

Loyalty Values: The Afghans and Americans both value loyalty, but develop these ties of loyalty in different directions. This difference has some corollary effects in other areas as well. The lashkar is to the tribe or qawm, and then to their personal charismatic leader. Occasionally these loyalties can conflict, splitting battle groups or qawm (TRADOC 2009). The battle groups of mujahidin that grew from the lashkars are similarly loyal to their leadership, and may not hold as strong a tie to their original locality, particularly if the group has been fighting for a long time, as military strongmen have used the war to increase their power (Giustozzi 2003). The tie of loyalty to an abstract central government is fragmented at best, and in many cases nonexistent. Where the loyalty does exist it is tied through personal connections, family, or simply the perception of advantage to be gained, such as money, supplies, and equipment. In this way the current GIRoA (Government of the Islamic Republic of Afghanistan) does not command the loyalty of warlords like Ismael Khan and Rashid Dostum, it allies with them (Dietl 2004). And in Afghanistan alliances are made to be broken when the battlefield calculus changes. Afghans warriors will likely not change sides to the disadvantage of their local community, family, or tribe. They will quite likely change sides to the disadvantage of a remote and disliked Kabul government. Permanent loyalty is reserved for those an individual personally knows and trusts. The current weakness of the Karzai regime offers the typical Afghan very little to attach permanent loyalty to even if he was inclined to give it (Lafraie 2009, 107).

54

This loyalty is also graduated in an interesting way. Kaplan described the mistrust that existed at the higher levels of the Pashtun leadership in Hizb-I-Islami. Abdul Haq was continually wary of entrusting other leaders within the organization with the details of his Kabul network. He had built it himself at great personal risk and effort. He used it for the good of the greater cause, but kept its details a closely held secret, even from members of his own family (Kaplan 1990, 72). Kaplan claimed that Haq, a Pashtun, trusted outsiders that he permitted into his inner circle more than he trusted his own family. This is not terribly unusual for tribal politics (TRADOC 2009). In Pashtun culture, a man's first cousin is a natural enemy due to inheritance conflict. Against an outside enemy, the tribe is a monolithic, indomitable foe. Inside the tribe the structure is an anarchic realist world order that requires Bismarkian skills to remain atop. This is one reason that Ghilzai Pashtun have been unable to compete with landed Durrani for political leadership in peacetime (Barfield 2007). This dynamic is also repeated within the Tajik, Uzbek, and Hazara dominated forces, where leaders faced competition or even betrayal from close subordinates.[18] Whether a leader is enormously popular, like Massoud, or ruthless in exacting revenge, like Dostum, they continually have to guard against usurpation. Tribal leadership is not an office codified by law, but tradition, and individual hold on that position is fragile (Barfield 2007).

In contrast, the US Military has a very strong loyalty to their legal central government, sealed by their traditional oath to support and defend the US Constitution, rather than an individual leader (The Center for Strategic and International Studies 2000,

---

[18]Rashid, *Taliban*, 57-58. General Dostum was ejected from his base in Mazar-E-Sharif in 1997 when his subordinate General Malik Pahlawan betrayed him to the Taliban.

7). The object of the loyalty is just as important as the loyalty itself. Hitler's Wermacht crossed a crucial threshold on the road to Nazi politicization and barbarism when they swore personal loyalty to the leader (Huntington 1957, 113). This was a marked difference form modern western professional military practice, where the soldier is loyal to the state.

In America's wars, the concept of changing sides in the middle of a battle does not exist. As it is for the state, subordinate units such as divisions or battalions cannot come and go as they choose, and certainly would not follow individual commanders if they chose to do so. The loyalty to an individual commander does not outweigh the legally defined loyalty to the state. Even in the American Civil War, Southern born officers like Robert E. Lee resigned their commissions with the US Army before joining the Confederate military. They did not take federal units with them in their defection, but organized them fresh from southern manpower. This allowed the institution of the US Army to survive the national fracturing of the Civil War (Huntington 1957, 213).

American Soldiers will most likely take this loyalty to the institution of the state for granted,[19] and may not understand the ANA soldier's conflicted loyalty to his home community, or his slow development of cohesion with people from different communities or ethnic groups. In turn, the ANA soldiers may have trouble giving unquestioning loyalty to a commander that they do not know and personally trust just because he holds a commission from Kabul. The commander in turn may have trouble trusting subordinates to carry out his instructions without strict supervision and detailed instructions that allow

---

[19]The Center for Strategic and International Studies, 65. In answer to a survey, 65 percent of US military agreed that most civilians had a great deal of respect for the US Armed Forces.

little to no initiative. If the officers in question served in the Soviet trained DRA military this tendency to micromanage may be even stronger (Koning 2009, 5).

US Soldiers may have trouble understanding dysfunction between Afghan commanders and their subordinate leaders and staff. US leaders lend their loyalty almost automatically to their unit commanders, as long as the orders given by those leaders are legal. Afghans have grown up in an anarchic, dangerous environment where trust cannot automatically be assumed. The organizations of the ANA and ANP are far too immature to guarantee the same level of loyalty between leaders and soldiers. Individual units may achieve some level of cohesion based on combat experience together, but new arrivals have to be vetted and proven, a continuous process.

This traditional distrust can affect the ability of leaders to mentor their subordinates. Leaders must be careful about revealing all of their secrets to their lieutenants, or they risk losing their value (Koning 2009, 5). Afghans may not share the US tradition of pride in a subordinate's success. Afghans may look at an empowered subordinate as a threat, rather than an asset, and resist training or passing on skills. This difference in attitude towards loyalty can also affect Afghan acceptance of western military organization and procedures, as well as the motivation towards combat.

Value of skills: Afghan warriors have historically been skilled fighters. Their marksmanship is mentioned as deadly throughout the 19th century. Mohamed Yousaf was favorably impressed with mujahidin performance at Pakistani training camps, which exceeded that of Pakistani soldiers. While that marksmanship appears to have declined considerably on the current Afghan battlefield, it has been replaced with explosives expertise. The holders of special skills are valued members of the tribe and battle group.

Skill provides social position and even rank. It lends personal power. Therefore a skill is personal property much the same as money or land. It is hardly something to be given away lightly. Therefore soldiers with unique qualifications may be reluctant to train others to their full potential. They may train assistants who can help with a complicated task, such as constructing an IED, but withhold certain technical details in order to cement their position of value.[20]

Similarly, an officer in the ANA may train their subordinate leaders sufficient military skills to enable them to competently follow orders, but not to take his position. Where US officers are taught that the highest success is to enable subordinates to maintain operating efficiency in their personal absence (Department of the Army 2006b, 3-12), Afghans would consider that a dangerous proposal to their personal authority. After all, if the subordinate can do the job then where is the value in the leader? This attitude comes directly from a lashkar mentality, where upward promotion is not guaranteed, and the position of battle group leader is essentially the ceiling of social promotion, and to be held against the challenge of subordinates.[21]

The US military attitude towards skill is that it is trainable. This attitude comes from the technological bent of the US way of war. Technical skills are by definition finite and transferable. This is possible due to the already high technical affinity of most

---

[20]Afsar Shahid A. and Christopher A. Samples. "The Evolution of the Taliban" (Thesis, Naval Post Graduate School, Monterey, CA, 2008). The Taliban pays by risk and results: $200 a month for a rifleman, $850 for planting an IED, $1000 for killing a foreigner, $2500 for killing a foreign soldier.

[21]Thomas Barfield, "Weapons of the not so Weak in Afghanistan: Pashtun Agrarian Structure and Tribal Organization for Times of War and Peace" (Research Study, Yale University, Agrarian Studies Colloquium Series, 2007), 6. The right to challenge for leadership is called tarbundi in Pashtun.

military recruits in the United States. Everything is trainable, and the leader's job is to teach and train as much as they can. Training and mentoring are considered to be core responsibilities of the leadership (Department of the Army 2006b). Leaders take pride in the success of junior soldiers that they have personally groomed and instructed. Because promotion upwards is scheduled, and lateral movement between units is common, subordinates who rise rapidly in the organization rarely pass their mentors. Therefore there is no risk to personal power or authority in teaching subordinates to the best of their ability to learn. On the contrary, the increased performance reflects positively on the leader.

For one example, marksmanship is a science that is systematically taught to all recruits, and sniper training is a higher level of that science. The M-16 series rifle has high standards of accuracy, and its manufacture is uniform, therefore all weapons function and shoot within a very narrow tolerance range. All soldiers have adequate vision to perform this task, with the proper correction. Techniques are taught to adjust the weapon to the shooter's eye systematically, so that virtually any rifle of the same model can be made theoretically accurate to the required 300 meters.

For the Afghan fighter, this skill is something different. The average AK-47 used by Afghan fighters, whether militia, Army, or Taliban, is an imprecise weapon. Adjustments to the front sight vary with manufacturing tolerances, because the AK-47s used in Afghanistan come from several different nations (Chivers, At War: Notes From the Front Line 2010). There is no systematic method for zeroing the weapon, only trial and error, or the acquired skill in adjusting sight picture to the weapon's variance. Formal training for ANA soldiers is rapid due to the urgent need to fill units (Younossi et al.

2009, 31), and their counterparts in the Taliban may receive no formal training in shooting whatsoever. In addition, with the limited medical care available in Afghanistan, many shooters are fighting with uncorrected vision problems. How many ANA soldiers or Taliban have been seen wearing glasses? This problem further limits the number of competent shooters in the battlefield (Chivers, At War: Notes From the Front Line 2010). The resulting handful of decent marksmen will naturally be valued, and may acquire special pay or equipment as a result. They will not likely be interested in transferring that skill that makes them special, and in some cases they may not be able to.

Attitudes towards organization and discipline: Afghan lashkars have a much different organization than US military units. Since the loyalty system is social rather than legal based the size and makeup of the lashkar or battle group is amoeba like. It is held together by the relationships and identity of tribe, family, or community. Mujahidin would describe their organization by naming the leader, stating the approximate number of fighters, and then list the equipment carried (Grau and Jalali 1996). There is almost never any mention of regular subordinate units such as squads or platoons. Even when the leaders of the mujahidin were previous Afghan army officers, their units are better described as groups of fighters (Grau and Jalali 1996, 157). Specialization of duty derived from unique skills or equipment brought or learned by the individual, who was therefore used to the best advantage, rather than an abstract position. The duties of the rest of the group would normally be ad hoc for each mission.[22]

---

[22]Grau and Jalali. In *On the Other Side of the Mountain*, mujahidin leaders usually give very detailed instructions to subordinate fighters, which is necessary when fighting is done by groups that lack Standard Operating Procedures or common training. Mujahidin leaders never mention a standard formation such as "squad" or "platoon" but

Leadership by personal example was important for mujahidin and Taliban alike. This is partially due to a requirement to periodically reassert leadership credentials (Barfield 2007, 6), and partly because the organization was not sufficiently developed to execute mission orders, but needed constant leadership and guidance. This dynamic tends to drive leaders to the front line and participate in particularly dangerous activities. Mujahidin General Zadran, a former Afghan army officer, talks about leading a single infantry squad of mujahidin on a captured tank when assaulting a government stronghold. Even though the "general" is in charge of a much larger force, the importance and danger of this mission compelled him to lead at the point of attack, rather than coordinating the operations of the entire force. In this example the general survived, but his force failed to capture the stronghold due to the failure of a supporting attack (Grau and Jalali 1996, 199-204).

Afghan leaders know the performance level of their organizations, and their position in combat tends to reflect the relative trust they have in their subordinates ability to lead in the absence of direct control. This method of control at the point of greatest impact is a tradition more in line with Alexander the Great than a modern military officer (Keegan 1988). Even experienced Afghan commanders describe two extremes: painstakingly detailed positioning of individual fighters, or careless direction that more often than not leads to fighters clumping or scattering at their discretion (Grau and Jalali 1996). In the first case the success of the mission is likely due to careful and time consuming reconnaissance, usage of terrain, and coordinated fires, but remains vulnerable to chance as the mujahidin command and control are incapable of

---

usually refer to other mujahidin groups by the name of the leader.

coordinating a response to changes on the battlefield (i.e. a sudden airlift of Soviet troops on unexpected terrain). In the second case the Afghan's natural initiative and fighting spirit are let loose, and the enemy may be confused by unconventional or unusual tactics and formations. The danger in loose swarms is that they can usually be defeated by a more cohesive and organized military unit unless aided by surprise.

In comparison, the US military officer is a manager, not executer, of violence, and he asserts his authority through his organization, which is highly defined (Huntington 1957). Orders given are systematically interpreted and executed in a manner that theoretically relieves the commander of the requirement to directly supervise each movement and action. The Commander relies on his subordinate leaders to issue orders in order to achieve his intent, and he does not need to specify each individual action to be taken (Department of the Army 2008, 3-29).

While Afghans may be extremely experienced fighters, they lack standardization, because specific tactics, techniques, and procedures are developed specific to each battle group. While these may be highly effective, they are not always interchangeable with other battle groups. In the Soviet war, different groups of mujahidin habitually had difficulty coordinating actions unless they had time for detailed discussion and planning, which in a very Afghan style, sound more like negotiations than planning conferences (Grau and Jalali 1996, 155).

Motivation for combat: The lashkar has a locally oriented martial tradition. While Afghans have a national identity, and have fought to maintain their independence, their goals for independence tended to orient around local and personal motivations. Massoud generated suspicion and resentment from the Pashtun party leaders when he negotiated a temporary cease fire with the Soviets (Kaplan 1990). This was purely pragmatic from Massoud's point of view, as he needed a respite from Soviet pressure on the Panshir valley. He either did not expect or did not overly care that his truce freed sparse Soviet mobile forces for action against other regions of the country, most noticeably the Pashtun south and east. Massoud's concern was primarily for the survival of his mujahidin and the marginal well being of the population of his valley.

Once again the difference in Afghan motivation to combat lies in where they place their loyalty. Since their loyalty is to their community or tribe, and inherently to themselves, they tend to define their objectives in local and personal terms. Most conflicts between Afghan families, clans, tribes, and communities today are over land and water rights (Dennys and Zaman 2009, 41). This is each micro society in effect acting as a tiny nation state. Many of these conflicts are resolved peacefully, but like with nations, military force by the lashkar is "always on the table." For individuals, the two most common motivations to resist the government in Afghanistan are anger at the government and lack of money (Afsar and Samples 2008).

The Pakistanis were continually frustrated by the various mujahidin motivations during the Soviet war. BG Yousaf complained that the mujahidin were stubborn, and resisted his attempts at operational coordination. In one case, where he identified a Soviet critical vulnerability in the fuel pipeline that supplied Bagram Airbase, he had considerable difficulty in convincing mujahidin commanders to attack the pipeline itself. Rather than sneak through guard posts and place explosive charges on the line, which would cause a disruption of Soviet air activities, mujahidin preferred to attack the guard posts directly. Yousaf explains that the mujahidin considered the sneak attack to be cowardly and personally unrewarding. The effect of disrupted fuel somewhere distant

held little value for a local mujahidin commander. He wanted excitement, personal glory

in battle, and loot. Therefore, the mujahidin would directly assault guard posts, and only

after destroying one would they place explosives on the line. They were more interested

in the equipment and credibility gained for their battle groups than in a greater objective

(Yousaf and Adkin 1992, 36).

This desire for personal notoriety as a famous fighter led to mujahidin taking

unnecessary risks out of a lack of tactical patience. The second Stinger attack in the

soviet war was a reckless shot against a high, fast moving jet fighter. The commander had

tired of waiting in ambush, and was in a race with a rival commander for the first Stinger

kill in Afghanistan. The commander's personal desire for glory overrode his guidance

and training, potentially degrading the operational surprise of Stingers in Afghanistan.

Later another mujahidin commander simply ignored all security guidelines by giving a

tell all interview about the Stingers to a reporter, and even allowed one to be

photographed (Yousaf and Adkin 1992, 176).

BG Yousaf coordinated operational missions in Afghanistan by appealing to

group commander's desires and needs. The mujahidin wanted weapons, supplies, and

special training from the Pakistanis. BG Yousaf traded these resources in exchange for

specific missions. Success led to more training and resources. He even systematically

controlled Stingers on the battlefield by requiring an empty launch tube for every fresh

resupply, in order to avoid black market leakage. The mujahidin practice of selling off

portions of their equipment, ammunition, or supplies in order to generate additional cash

was an open secret that the Pakistanis tried to control but never eliminated. Captured

Soviet equipment literally became loot that was transferrable to cash for the commander, particularly for rare Soviet souvenirs sold to journalists in Peshawar (Yousaf and Adkin 1992).

One universal motivation for Afghans to fight is defending their faith. Since the Taraki regime and later DRA versions were communist and therefore atheist, the conservative reaction developed out of religious as well as traditional outrage (Edwards 1987, 34-37). In both of the British invasions, the religious leadership declared resistance to be a duty of faithful Muslims, and therefore fighters gained personal salvation through combat(Grissom 2009). This religious fervor was increased exponentially during the 1980s, as Soviet brutality and repression provided an enemy that was positively satanic from the Afghan viewpoint (Magnus 1987). However defending the faith is evidently not quite a strong enough motivation to erase the desire to compete with rival lashkar or tribes.[23]

Another universal motivation for Afghans to fight, enacted on a personal level, is revenge. In pashtunwali this is an imperative that is required in order to maintain tribal or family honor, which is another way of terming the street credibility in the community (TRADOC 2009, 10). Loss of honor means that other tribes may scent weakness, and move to take land and other resources. This revenge imperative is called badal (Gant 2009), and the Soviets generated an unlimited amount with their deliberate campaign of depopulation of the Afghan countryside and the resulting 1 million deaths. Many

---

[23]Yousaf, and Adkin. The Afridi Pashtun on the Pakistan border had no compunctions about accepting Soviet and DRA money and weapons in return for raiding mujahidin supply movements (Kaplan 1990). The conflict between Heknatyr and Massoud's forces at the time of the battle for Jalalabad has also already been described.

mujahidin were motivated by a strong personal desire for revenge against the Soviets (Kaplan 1990). ISAF forces therefore risk a similar response, even though on a smaller scale, as a result of collateral damage from air and artillery strikes.

US forces are motivated by a variety of factors that ultimately tie into a national strategic objective. Even though individual soldiers may enlist out of personal goals, they tend to modify those goals so that they match or supplement the unit's mission. The unit is required by the orders process to nest its mission objectives with the mission and intent of the unit one and two levels up. This continues up the chain of command until the unit is supporting specific directives from the President of the United States. US Soldiers generally do not modify their mission out of personal interest nor conduct it specifically to gain personal advantage. To do so would be considered a serious ethical and legal violation. Leaders identify personal goals of advancement through their organization's success; therefore it is to their best interest to accomplish their assigned missions efficiently.

On a national scale Americans are most comfortable with total objectives in wartime. Traditionally Americans avoided limited warfare, as any objective short of an existential threat was not worth going to war over, and existential threats required a full national effort to fight (Lewis 2007, 22). This tradition was most firmly realized in World War II, and was increasingly degraded by the various cold war conflicts and interventions. The Weinberger-Powell Doctrine temporarily resurrected the traditional American view of war's ideal objectives and related intensity, but rapidly faded in the face of a series of limited deployments in the 1990s (Bacevich 2005).

Even in limited wars, such as the current conflicts in Iraq and Afghanistan, the US military strives to articulate relevant, measureable goals to define success that directly support national strategic objectives. The military structures its conditions of success in such a way that even the smallest tactical action, and its potential cost of American life, can be justified in terms of these national goals (Lewis 2007, 34). Afghans tend to fight for more immediate and personal objectives, such as revenge, loot, or to defend the community. Defending the community may be a motivation the United States and Afghan fighters share, yet the typical US soldier would reject out of hand a combat action intended solely to benefit his unit or its leadership. Because both cultures define mission accomplishment in such starkly different terms, it will take considerable effort to translate the ISAF mission in a meaningful way to an Afghan tribe. Major Gant started his explanation by showing a video of the 11 September attacks. The mission to fight al Qaeda was explicable to the tribal leader in terms of revenge (Gant 2009). In this situation, it is unlikely that Major Gant would have made much impression if he had tried to explain the partially altruistic motivation of the US' aggressive spread of democracy in the "non integrating gap" in order to "enhance globalization" and the eventual "end of history."

The final chapter will summarize the conclusions developed in this chapter, and explain the implications of cultural conflict in the United States' training, equipping, and organizing of the ANA. Further, the conclusion will suggest some bridging strategies the can utilize shared cultural values to overcome the cultural gaps between the two martial cultures.

CHAPTER 5

CONCLUSION

Afghan and US martial cultures conflict and share in practices, history, and values. This comparative study of Afghan and US martial cultures has revealed key contrasts in values towards loyalty, skill transference, organization, and motivation for combat. Out of these loyalty is the most important because a uniquely Afghan attitude of loyalty or lack thereof, prevents the institutional trust and cooperation that a western meritocratic military system relies on. Afghan and US soldiers will share values on personal courage, respect for skill, and equality of sacrifice. Both cultures represent two different but also quite successful military traditions at the dawn of the 21st century.

The relationship between the US Military and ANA in the continuing struggle to establish a stable central government will be greatly defined by the potential to merge these two martial cultures. The last experiment of an Afghan army developed by a foreign power, the Soviet sponsored DRA Army, was a failure of military effectiveness and civil military relations. The Soviet practice of war was highly centralized and firepower focused, which negated many of the inherent advantages of the Afghan fighter's physical and moral courage, individuality, initiative, and small group loyalty. The DRA Army also suffered from Afghan habits of corruption, factional struggles, and suspicion. The result was an organization as ill suited to the Afghan society as the government it proposed to represent. The DRA government was never accepted by the great majority of the population, and increased Soviet military activity against the population generated fear and hatred but not compliance (Magnus 1987, 196). The DRA

68

was a lesser partner in its own national civil war. It never developed into a national institution. Without outside support, it was unable to continue fighting even for survival.

In order to avoid these mistakes CSTC-A trainers and mentors need to develop ANSF development goals understanding the inherent strengths and weaknesses of Afghan culture. Trainers coming back from Afghanistan have described the ANA as generally very brave, though sometimes to a fault, and very capable fighters (Clinton 2007). They have reported problems with discipline, recording that absenteeism, with or without permission, are a significant problem in maintaining the strength in a kandak (Boesen 2008). The loyalty and cohesiveness of leaders is also a recurrent problem. ANA officers come from a variety of backgrounds, and in some cases former DRA officers and mujahidin are serving together (Schroeder 2007). Because of Afghanistan's tradition of changeable loyalties, this is more acceptable than in some other nations that have fought long civil wars. However, many officers favor subordinates for personal loyalty, which is often supplemented by corruption and hoarding of supplies (US DoD Inspector General 2009, 25). The promotion system is widely criticized to be driven by nepotism and familial, financial, or tribal relationships rather than meritocracy (Haynes 2009). The ANA is still driven by Afghan ideas of loose organization, which means that the supply system works when it wants to, and hides behind Soviet style inflexibility when it does not (Schroeder 2007).

Successful mentorship of Afghan soldiers relies on cultural understanding and communication skills that have been discussed in detail in other studies and training products (Poitras 2009). This study is of the merging of cultural traditions and values that will inevitably occur when US trainers work with Afghan soldiers. The thesis identified some conflicts, but also some shared values, and it is in these shared values that we may be able to identify strategies to overcome the potential conflicts in order to avoid a cultural train wreck.

How can CSTC-A overcome these conflicts? The Afghan and US martial cultures value courage, military skill, and shared sacrifice. US Embedded Training Teams, Special Forces, and mentoring units have met success in the past by capitalizing on these shared values. In turn the trust and respect earned can encourage stubborn Afghan fighters to consider adopting new methods of organization and training. Over time the success of the ANA organization and its credibility will grow identity and attract loyalty (Baker 2004, 5). This will take a considerable amount of time and even more patience.

The US embedded training team, as an outsider, has a role to play as a trusted confident for the Afghan commander. Once the American soldier has earned the Afghan's trust, he will be in some ways closer than the commander's subordinates. Being naturally suspicious, the commander may never trust his subordinates from undermining and potentially replacing him (TRADOC 2009). The American likely does not have any interest in promotion within the ANA, so he is a safer risk for confidence. Once accepted, US soldiers can serve as a bridge between Afghan leaders, and through the Provincial Reconstruction team, to the civilian government. US soldiers in this role can facilitate exchange of information and resources in a way that may initially feel safer for Afghan leaders who have not developed a working relationship. It is important to remember that the trusted outsider cannot usurp his counterpart's authority. This can be hard for some type A personality US officers who are intent on making the ANA perform to US Standard Army Training System.

The first step to success in training an indigenous military force is developing rapport. This is never more important than when working with Afghans. All ETT and SOF soldiers have explained the importance of social relations with their counterpart.[24] This study suggests that the relationship will be greatly strengthened through actions in addition to drinking tea and chatting. Operating in the field, Afghan units and trainers in combat will develop mutual respect for each other's bravery under fire. A trainer who obviously hangs back and avoids danger that Afghan soldiers would habitually ignore will not generate credibility or trust with his counterparts. On the contrary, such action may bring back memories of Soviet mistreatment of the DRA Army. Trainers who willingly face danger in the course of their duty will be seen as fellow warriors that are worthy of respect. An example of how quickly performance can degrade when the mentors lack credibility can be seen in Operation Anaconda. The Afghan militia forces quickly lost heart in their US SOF mentors when promised air support failed to appear on the battlefield, leading to a rapid retreat in the face of Al Qaeda indirect fire (Naylor 2005).

Trainers can also develop credibility through sharing hardship with their ANA counterparts. When possible, the US soldiers should be where the ANA is, particularly when conditions are difficult. If the weather is harsh, and the terrain tough, vehicles are breaking down, and food is short, US trainers should be share the difficulty, and share

---

[24]Major Jim Gant, *One Tribe at a Time.* Los Angeles, California: Nine Sisters Imports, Inc., 2009. Major Gant spent hours discussing personal issues and small talk with his tribal chief counterpart before he began to coordinate operations. LTC John Schroeder, Interview by John McCool, Operational Leadership Experiences, *Interview with LTC John Schroeder* (Fort Leavenworth, KS: Combat Studies Institute, 16 February). Lieutenant Colonel Schroeder devoted his first meeting with a former DRA officer to establishing personal relationships.

personal resources when possible. This is not to suggest that US Soldiers should attempt to out tough Afghans. This would be highly unfair to the Americans, and would likely lead to most of the ETT personnel incapacitated. Afghans take for granted that they can endure more than westerner, correctly evaluating the effect of higher standards of living in the United States and European Union. What counts is that trainers try to share some of Afghanistan's lifestyle while they are there. This willingness to share some of the burden will also generate trust and respect.

US soldiers have much more military technical skill than Afghan soldiers, due to their civilian and military education. The experienced Afghan fighter may have superior abilities to evaluate and negotiate terrain, use cover and concealment, and move under fire. He is also not likely to understand the mechanics of zeroing his rifle, read maps, nor write orders (Younossi et al. 2009). As discussed, due to the Afghan habit of jealously protecting leadership positions, the ANA soldier's leaders may not be inclined to teach him. In this case the US trainer, as the trusted outside agent, can facilitate the mentorship of junior soldiers, ensuring that the senior, more experienced leadership is transferring their skills to the younger generation while retaining their authority and position. The US trainer can help the entire organization by conducting universal skills training that unarguably help the entire unit, such as marksmanship, vehicle maintenance, and map reading. IN practice much of this training can be used to develop planning and leadership skills in the junior officer and NCO corps. The trainer can conduct "special" training for the leadership that emphasizes military arts, planning, and command relationships, which will enhance the leader's stature.

In particular the value of literacy to the ANA and ANP cannot be overestimated. The Afghan national literacy rate is less than 30 percent (Younossi et al. 2009). In this society education has taken a back seat to survival skills. Yet the ability to read and write orders and reports for officers and NCOs is critical for a well organized military. The current programs that incorporate basic literacy into ANA education programs should be emphasized and sustained throughout the ANA soldier's career. As soon as conditions permit, the ANA private should be initiated to literacy and mathematics as well. This will make the ex ANA soldier a man of great stature when he returns to his community, which will only serve to raise that of the ANA in Afghan society. Ultimately raising the level of education in the ANSF will benefit the entire nation as well as aid the force to become more efficient. This will present a sharp contrast between young men who join the ANA and become literate and young men who join the Taliban and become suicide bombers.[25]

The ETT can utilize its command and control capabilities to help the ANA officers empower their subordinates. The ETT chief can reassure an ANA officer that a promising Afghan sergeant can be entrusted with an independent mission because he is accompanied by one of the ETT's NCO's. This is another method where the outsider as trusted agent can facilitate growth in the Afghan organization.

The trainers must understand that even if their relationship with their counterpart Afghan unit resembles a tribal alliance, it is the growth of a modern military institution. If

---

[25]Matthew Dearing, "Examining the Suicide Terror Movement in Afghanistan," *Culture & Conflict Review* 2, no. 3 (Summer): 1-16. Most failed suicide bombers are poor, illiterate, and lack awareness of politics outside their community. In one case a young man captured before his mission was completed expected a financial reward *after* completing his suicide bomb attack. Most bombers were motivated by a powerful desire to benefit their community.

Afghanistan is to develop a functioning central government, it will need an army that it can rely on (A. A. Jalali 2002). This will mean a significant but necessary change in a core cultural value. Developing a military culture that prizes loyalty to an ambiguous nation of Afghanistan in addition to and in precedence over tribal and local loyalties will not happen in ten years. Changing the Afghan warrior's culture of loyalty to qawm to include the ideal of state service requires individual Afghans to cut loose fundamental understandings that they rely on for safety and security in a violent society. An effort of this magnitude will require significant willingness to change from the mass of Afghan soldiers. It is unknown if they are even aware of challenge that is being asked of them and the implications for their countries future that follow on their success of failure.

The fundamental question of where the Afghan fighter's loyalty will rest after ISAF inevitably leaves is being decided now within the ranks of the ANA. The military institution may be the forum for Afghans to develop trust and respect across regional, tribal, and ethnic lines. If it fails in this task then the ANA may fragment under pressure and collapse into warlord factions oriented on regional and ethnic loyalties once again. ETTs training ANA kandaks and SF ODAs working with tribal lashkar must help these two institutions to work together, and not strengthen one at the expense of the other. Neither is going away. The ISAF force as a whole, as that trusted outside agent, needs to coordinate its actions across the entire security environment. Ultimately all actions must orient towards reinforcing the authority of the Kabul government.

There is currently a debate of the strategy for successful stability within Afghanistan. All observers recognize that a large foreign military presence in Afghanistan generates hostility within the population over time. In order for the GIRoA to secure its authority, it must rely on an Afghan, not foreign force. Yet this force must be culturally acceptable to the society, or it will not be recognized as legitimately Afghan (Lewis 2007, 8). The current debate centers on the relative power of the central army versus local tribal lashkars. Some argue that the central Kabul government has never maintained the monopoly on organized violence over the nation, and that its army has never been more than a personal militia for the king or president (Gant 2009). The other side argues that a strong national army is essential for Afghanistan's future development as a modern nation state, and that only centralized identity formed around the army can unify the nation after chaos for so long. Furthermore, several studies cited in this research cast doubt on the strength of tribal institutions remaining in Afghanistan after the tremendous damage inflicted by the DRA, Soviets, and Taliban.[26]

The appeal to tribes can be deceptive. As noted in this study, not all qawms are, in fact tribes, though the martial culture of the lashkar may be similar, qawms in fact are not. They are best described as micro societies that may be tribes and sometimes act tribal, but often are local communities, families, or other identities (Wegener 2007). In addition, where a Pashtun tribe may be strong enough in one district to repel the Taliban insurgency with ISAF assistance, this is not true for qawms across the country. There is also the distinct possibility that qawms may choose to support the Taliban for their own

---

[26]Lieutenant Andrew Wegener, *A Complex and Changing Dynamic: Afghan Responses to Foreign Intervention* (Canberra: Land Warfare Studies Center); Antonio Giustozzi, "Respectable Warlords? The Politics of State-building in Post-Taleban Afghanistan" (Research report, Development Research Center LSE, London, 2003); TRADOC, G2 Human Terrain System. Wegener, Giustozzi, and the TRADOC Human Terrain Team all describe the process where the Soviet and Taliban wars devastated tribal structure by death and mass dislocation, and fostered their replacement by military and religious authorities.

specific reasons, including opium cultivation and trade, religious loyalty, resentment of the Kabul government and foreign forces, or simply monetary reward.

Tribes and other micro societies in Afghanistan cannot be ignored in the security strategy for Afghanistan. The future success of Afghanistan over the Taliban lies in an alliance between the Kabul government and the local communities. The central army has a key role in this strategy. It is generally respected in Afghan society, more so than any other institution, including the Afghan National Police (ANP) (Afsar and Samples 2008). It is developing a credible fighting capability; particularly since US funding and manning have drastically increased since 2006. But it cannot be everywhere at one time, and will rely on local lashkar to provide intelligence and supplement fighting power. This alliance has successfully defended the nation in the past against the British. It is up to the government and military leadership to successfully make the case that this alliance is in the best interest of the qawms. Evidence suggests that in Taliban controlled areas, particularly in Pashtun majority qawms, they have not made the case (International Crisis Group 2003).

Much of the future loyalty and culture of the ANA will be determined by the evolving character of the Afghan national government in Kabul. It will be difficult for the ANA to transfer its loyalty to a government that does not deserve that loyalty. It will also be difficult for ANA soldiers to risk their lives in the field for the future security of Kabul if they see the city as a Karzai family fiefdom (Lafraie 2009, 107).

If the United States truly wants to leave behind a capable and trustworthy ANA that will form the backbone of Afghanistan, it will have to realistically asses the objectives for success against the time allotted to complete the mission. The ANA may be as tactically proficient as it is going to become working under a westernized structure without cultural value changes. The next question may be to modify the structure of the ANA, how it fights, and how it coordinates its security operations with lashkars. The findings of this study suggest that the ANA cannot simply adopt the American model of organization without significant allowance for practices that would otherwise considered unacceptable in western armies. The problems of loyalty, discipline, and motivation may be so deep that even a modified westernized model will require significant patience and perseverance to realize. Even reduced western expectations are unlikely to be met by the current presidential deadline of summer of 2011 for the initiation of ISAF's drawdown.

This study has developed a modest step in fully understanding the strategic implications of the cultural contrasts between American and Afghan martial cultures. This research developed a theoretical model of Afghan martial culture and described some implications on the current strategy employed by CSTC-A. The next steps would include a comprehensive survey from the field that gathers quantitative data that would validate assumptions developed in this thesis. Validated assumptions combined with tactics, techniques, and procedures for bridging cultural gaps between martial cultures should then be distributed to all American ETTS, partnering units, and ODAs. The final step would be a close examination of CSTC-A stated objectives and metrics for ANA development, in order to determine whether the current definition of success for the ANA is realistic within the expected lifetime of CSTC-A's mission.

REFERENCE LIST

Afsar, Shahid A., and Christopher A. Samples. 2008. The evolution of the taliban. Thesis, Naval Post Graduate School, Monterey, CA.

Anderson, Jon Lee. 2002. *The lion's grave.* New York, NY: Grove Press.

Bacevich, Andrew. 2005. *The new American militarism: How Americans are seduced by war.* Oxford: Oxford University Press.

Baker, LTC Mary A. 2004. Winning the peace? An examination into building an Afghan National Army (ANA) and New Iraqi Army (NIA). Research Project, U.S. Army War College, Carlisle Barracks, Pennsylvania.

Barfield, Thomas. 2007. Weapons of the not so weak in Afghanistan: Pashtun agrarian structure and tribal organization for times of war and peace. Research Study, Yale University, Agrarian Studies Colloquium Series.

Boesen, MAJ Steve. 2008. Interview by CPT Shawn O'Brien. Operational Leadership Experiences. *Interview with MAJ Stephen Boesen.* Fort Leavenworth, KS: Combat Studies Institute, 7 July.

Center for Strategic and International Studies. 2000. *American military culture in the twenty-first century.* Washington, DC: The Center for Strategic and International Studies.

Chivers, C.J. 2010a. Afghan marksmen forget the fables. *At War: Notes from the Front lines.* 26 March. http://atwar.blogs.nytimes.com/2010/03/26/afghan-marksmen-forget-the-fables/ (accessed 30 April 2010).

———. 2010b. Afghan marksmanship pointing not aiming. *At War: Notes From the Front Line.* 9 April. http://atwar.blogs.nytimes.com/2010/04/09/afghan-marksmanship-pointing-not-aiming/ (accessed 30 April 2010).

———. 2010c. A first hand look at figherfighters in Marja. *At War: Notes From the Front Line.* 19 April. http://atwar.blogs.nytimes.com/2010/04/19/a-firsthand-look-at-firefights-in-marja/ (accessed 30 April 2010).

———. 2010d. Putting taliban sniper fire in context. *At War: Notes from the front lines.* 19 April. http://atwar.blogs.nytimes.com/2010/04/20/putting-taliban-sniper-fire-in-context/ (accessed 30 April 2010).

Clinton, Jr., MAJ Thomas 2007. Interview by MAJ Conrad Harvey. Operational Leadership Experiences. *Interview with MAJ Thomas Clinton Jr.* Fort Leavenworth, KS: Combat Studies Institute, 12 March.

Cordesman, Anthony H. 2009. *Shaping afghan national security forces: What it will take to implement Obama's new strategy.* Washington, DC: Center for Strategic and International Studies.

Dearing, Matthew. 2008. Examining the suicide terror movement in Afghanistan. *Culture & Conflict Review* 2, no. 3 (Summer): 1-16.

Defence Manpower Data Center. 2010. Casualties by type. 3 April. https://www.dmdc.osd.mil/appj/dwp/getLinks.do?category=dod&tab=3 (accessed 5 April 2010).

Dennys, Christian, and Idrees Zaman. 2009. Trends in local Afghan conflicts. Conflict Analysis Paper, Cooperation for Peace and Unity (CPAU).

Department of the Army. 2005. Field Manual 1, *The Army.* Washington, DC: Headquarters, Department of the Army.

———. 2008. Field Manual 3-0, *Operations.* Washington, DC: Department of the Army.

———. 2006a. Field Manual 3-24, *Counterinsurgency.* Washington, DC: Headquarters, Department of the Army.

———. 2006b. Field Manual 6-22, *Army leadership.* Washington, DC: Headquarters, Department of the Army.

Dietl, Gulshan. 2004. War, peace, and the warlords: The case of Ismail Khan in Herat. *Alternatives: Turkish journal of international relations*, 3, no. 2&3 (Summer/Fall): 41-66.

Edwards, Davis Busby. 1987. Origins of the anti-Soviet jihad. In *Afghan Resistance: The Politics of Survival*, by Grant M. Farr and John G. Merriam, 21-51. Boulder, CO: Westview Press.

Feifer, Gregory. 2009. *The great gamble.* New York, NY: Harper Collins Publishers.

Gant, Major Jim. 2009. *One tribe at a time.* Los Angeles, California: Nine Sisters Imports, Inc.

Giustozzi, Antonio. 2003. Respectable warlords? The politics of state-building in post-Taleban Afghanistan. Research report, Development Research Center LSE, London.

Goodson, Dr. Larry. 2004. Winning the peace? An examination into building an Afghan National Army (ANA) and New Iraqi Army (NIA). Strategy Research Project, U.S. Army War College, Carlisle Barracks, PA.

Grau, Lester. 2005. *The bear went over the mountain.* Washington, DC: National Defense University Press, 2005.

Grau, Lester, and Ahmed Ali Jalali. 1996. *The other side of the mountain.* Quantico, VA: United States Marine Corps Studies.

Grissom, Michael T. 2009. Teutoburg forest, Little Bighorn, and Maiwand: Why superior forces sometimes fail. Master's thesis, Command and General Staff College, Ft. Leavenworth, KS.

Haug, MAJ Jan Erik. 2009. The Operational Mentoring and Liaison Team program as a model for assisting the development of an effective Afghan National Army. Master's thesis, Command and General Staff College, Ft. Leavenworth, KS.

Haynes, Jeff. 2009. Reforming the Afghan National Army: Getting the most out of the ANA, so we can do Less. Foreign Policy Research Institute.

Hillen, John. 1999. Must US military culture change? *Parameters* (Fall).

Hofstede, Geert Jan. 2005. *Cultures and organizations: Software of the mind.* New York, NY: McGraw Hill.

Hoskins, MAJ Brant D. 2007. Religion and other cultural variables in modern operational environments. Monograph, School of Advanced Military Studies, Fort Leavenworth, KS.

Huntington, Samuel B. 1957. *The soldier and the state.* Toronto: Vintage Books.

International Crisis Group. 2003. Afghanistan: The problem of Pashtun alienation. Think Tank Research Project, Kabul/Brussels.

Jalali, Ali A. 2002. Rebuilding Afghanistan's National Army. *Parameters* (Autumn): 72-86.

Jalali, Ali A., and Lester Grau. 1999. Night stalkers and mean streets: Afghan urban guerillas. *Infantry* (January-April).

Kaplan, Robert. 1990. *Soldiers of God: With islamic warriors in Afghanistan and Pakistan.* New York, NY: Vintage Books.

Keegan, John. 1988. *The mask of command.* Penguin Books.

Kipling, Rudyard. 1900. *Early verse.* New York: Charles Scribner's Sons.

Knox, MacGregor and Murray, Williamson. 2001. *The dynamics of military revolution.* Cambridge: Cambridge University Press.

Koning, LCOL D.A. de. 2009. *Mentoring of the ANSF.* Topic Lessons Report, Ontario, Canada: Army Lessons Learned Center (Canada).

Lafraie, Najibullah. 2009. Resurgence of the Taliban insurgency in Afghanistan. *International Politics* 46, no. 1: 102-113.

Lewis, Adrian R. 2007. *The American culture of war.* New York, London: Routledge.

MacGregor, MG Sir Charles Metcalfe. 1985. *War in Afghanistan, 1878-80.* Detroit: Wayne State University Press.

Magnus, Ralph H. 1987. Humanitarian response to an inhuman strategy. In *Afghan Resistance*, by Grant M. Farr and John G. Merriam, 191-212. Boulder, CO: Westview Press, Inc.

Mashack, Major Trahan T. 2009. Developing a self-sustaining Afghan National Army. Monograph, School of Advanced Military Studies, Ft. Leavenworth, KS.

McGirk, Tim. 2010. A civil war among Afghanistan's Insurgents? *Time.* 6 March.

Meyer, Karl. 2003. *The dust of empire.* London, UK: Abacus.

Milli, Haydar, and Jacob Townshend. 2009. Tribal Dynamics of the Afghanistan and Pakistan Insurgencies. *CTC Sentinel (Combating Terrorism Center at West Point)* (August): 7-10.

Naylor, Sean. 2005. *Not a good day to die.* New York, NY: Berkley Books.

Neamatollah, Nojumi, Dyan Mazurana, and Elizabeth Stites. 2009. *Life and security in rural Afghanistan.* Plymouth, UK: Rowman & Littlefield Publishers, INC.

Pape, Major Jason M. 2009. How the Army resists change. Monograph, School of Advanced Military Studies, Ft. Leavenworth, KS.

Parker, Geoffrey, ed. 2005. *The Cambridge history of warfare.* Cambrdge University Press: Cambridge.

Poitras, MAJ Maurice V. 2009. Adoptable customs or practices in a military operations environment. Monograph, School of Advanced Military Studies, Ft. Leavenworth, KS.

Rashid, Ahmed. 2010. Interview by Terry Gross and NPR Fresh Air. *Ahmed Rashid offers ad update on the Taliban.* 17 February.

———. 2000. *Taliban.* New Haven: Yale University Press.

Record, Jeffrey.2007. *Beating Goliath: Why insurgencies win.* Washington DC: Potomic Books, Inc.

Roy, Olivier. 1991. The lessons of the Soviet Afghan war. Oxford: Institute for Strategic Studies.

Sale, Lady Florentia. 1969. *A journal of the First Afghan War*. Oxford: Oxford University Press.

Schein, Edgar. 1990. Organizational Culture. *American Psychologist* (February).

Schroeder, LTC John. 2007. Interview by John McCool. Operational Leadership Experiences. *Interview with LTC John Schroeder*. Fort Leavenworth, KS: Combat Studies Institute, 16 February.

Taylor, Richard L. 2005. Tribal alliances: Ways, means, and ends to successful strategy. Research paper, Strategic Studies Institute, Carlisle Barracks, PA.

Thomas, Lowell. 1925. *Beyond Khyber Pass*. New York, NY: The Century Company.

Titunik, Regina F. 2008. The myth of the macho military. *Polity* (April): 137-163.

TRADOC. G2 Human Terrain System. 2009. My cousin's enemy is my friend: A study of Pashtun "tribes" in Afghanistan. Afghanistan Research Center White Paper, Fort Leavenworth: United States Army.

US Inspector General. 2009. *Report on the assessment of US and coalition plans to train, equip, and field the Afghan National Security Forces*. Washington, DC: US Departement of Defense.

Wegener, Lieutenant Andrew. 2007. *A complex and changing dynamic: Afghan responses to foreign intervention*. Canberra: Land Warfare Studies Center.

Weigley, Russel. 1973. *The American way of war: A history of United States military strategy and policy*. Bloomington: Indiana University Press.

Wood, David. 2010. Afghanistan who are we fighting for, anyway after eight years, strategy Is still unclear. *Politics Daily*. 9 February. Politics Daily.htm (accessed 22 April 2010).

Younossi, Obaid, Peter Dahl, Dohl Peter Thruelsen, Jonathon Vaccaro, Jerry M Sollinger, and Grady Brian. 2009. *The long march building an Afghan Army*. Santa Monica, CA: Rand Corporation.

Yousaf, Mohammed, and Mark Adkin. 1992. *The battle for Afghanistan*. Yorkshire: Pen and Sword.